Walking with Elijah

The Fable of a Life Journey and a Fulfilled Soul

Doobie Shemer

Copyright © 2014 by Doobie Shemer
All rights reserved.
ISBN-13:978-0-9913494-4-9
ISBN-10: 099134944X
Library of Congress Control Number: TXu 1-919-061

About the Author

Doobie Shemer's incredible life journey began in his birthplace, Kibbutz Givat-Brener, Israel. Yearning to explore life's meanings, he has travelled widely and experienced many cultures—mystical India, beautiful Cyprus—before making his home in California, where he is now a practicing shamanism, journeying for others.

Please contact Doobie if you are looking for insight or a revelation about personal challenges, professional obstacles, or relationship issues by submitting your question using the link below:

http://walkingwithelijah.com/ask-elijah
http://www.doobieshemer.com/

Acknowledgments:

Heartfelt gratitude to Grandma Tova for showing me what real courage looks like, to my mother Elizabeth for teaching me to question, and to my dad Haim for guiding me from heaven.

I am humbled and grateful to my dear friend Dana for introducing me to shamanism, and to my beloved wife Vicky for her inspiration and love.

Thanks to Esther Bradley-DeTally for guidance and support, to my editor Averill Buchanan, and to graphic designer Zackary, at Raven Tree Design, for my cover design and chapter illustrations.

~Doobie

Contents

Preface: Writing the Book _____ vii

Introduction: Kibbutz—Growing up in Paradise _____ ix

Chapter One: Are You My Teacher? _____ 1
   Dolphin, the Power Animal _____ 4
   Hilla, the Spiritual Guide _____ 9
   Elijah, the Teacher _____ 13

Chapter Two: What Else is Up There? _____ 17
   Bear, my other Power Animal _____ 17
   Yellow _____ 20
   Blue, Green, Red _____ 22

Chapter Three: A Life Journey _____ 25
   Grandma Tova _____ 25
   Dying and Beyond _____ 30
   Dad _____ 33
   "Your Son is Your Father" _____ 34

Chapter Four: Mind, Body, and Soul _____ 41
   "What Happened to Sharon?" _____ 41
   Controller, Carrier, and Passenger _____ 44

Chapter Five: Love and Souls _____ 51
   Love _____ 53
   Soul Mates _____ 55
   Destiny _____ 56
   Plain Souls _____ 57
   Angels _____ 58
   Prophets _____ 58

Chapter Six: The Ten Soul Commandments _____ **61**
   First and Second Soul Commandments _____ *66*
   Third Soul Commandment _____ *67*
   Fourth Soul Commandment _____ *67*
   Fifth - Tenth Soul Commandments _____ *68*

Chapter Seven: Role of the Complementing Opposites _____ **71**
   "The New World": Symphony No. 9 (Dvořák) _____ *71*
   Adagio _____ *74*
   Largo _____ *75*
   Scherzo _____ *76*
   Allegro _____ *77*

Chapter Eight: Divining the Truth _____ **81**
   Divination _____ *82*
   Red World _____ *86*
   "At the End You Will Reach the Beginning" _____ *89*

Also by Doobie Shemer: _____ **93**
Connect with Doobie: _____ **94**
About the Author _____ **95**

Preface:
Writing the Book

~~~ — ~~~

Hilla and I were sitting on the beach in the Lower World. We were watching Dolphin, swimming around, keeping one eye on us. She silently reached out to hold my hand.

"Hilla, we spoke about writing a book," I said. "I want to put everything in writing, to help people understand what life is, to explain love and friendship, why it is the way it is. I would like to share with others what it is really like, the way I see life."

"Of course," she said. "You will, don't worry. However, one thing you need to learn—you can't rush these things. You'll get it done when you're ready, not a minute before."

"You're right, I guess," I replied quietly.

We were silent for a while. Dolphin approached us. I could see the curve of his sleek gray back as he tried to keep himself above the water to catch our conversation.

"Let's talk about my book please," I said.

"Sure," she said and looked at me, smiling, her brown-green eyes sparkling.

"What should be the theme of the book?"

"Well, we've been going to Elijah," she said. "I don't know what he would want to talk about, what he would like to share with you, so let's just not plan it. We'll continue going to Elijah, and every time we go, it might be a new chapter, a new story. At the end you'll find out that there is some sort of connection between the chapters."

"Okay, let's see how that goes," I said.

"Elijah will help. He will guide you."

We sat in silence for a while, looking at the emerald water and at Dolphin.

"I can see you have doubts," she said, reading my mind as usual. "You want to write a book for people to enjoy, to have fun," she went on. "But that isn't what you'll write it for. Your book will make people think. It will help those that have been looking for directions and answers. You'll not write to please them."

And indeed I did.

Walking with Elijah is a collection of shamanic journeys I have experienced with my Teacher, Elijah the Prophet. Each chapter tells about a journey that relates to different aspects of existence.

When I start a shamanic journey, a topic or question appears in my mind. I do not try to second-guess or predict it; nor do I expect specific answers. I receive unpredictable and surprising answers.

Dear reader, shamanic journeys bring me deep pleasure and it is my sincere wish that this will be your experience, too, as you read *Walking with Elijah*.

Thank you.

Yours truly,
Doobie.

Introduction:

Kibbutz—Growing up in Paradise

Those of you who grew up in a kibbutz, as I did, will probably agree with me that a kibbutz is nothing but a children's paradise. Those of you who weren't that lucky, just imagine growing up in nature's temple, where your playground includes a gigantic field of green grass, groves of oranges, lemons, avocados and other kinds of fruits, a forest of towering eucalyptus trees, and where the fragrance of jasmine bushes constantly hangs in the air. Imagine a place where the most common transportation is a few tractors, horses, mules, and a couple of donkeys. You don't fear cars racing on the roads; in fact, there are no asphalt roads at all except the main entrance. Only dirt roads connect the kibbutz's different sections—members' houses, the school area, the industrial zone, the cattle barns, the groves.

The kibbutz was a place where during the day all you could hear was the sound of children playing and birds singing, and during the night a random hungry baby crying, accompanied by symphonies of crickets and the odd lonely wolf howling to the moon. That was the stage setting of my life and the soundtrack of my childhood.

In the kibbutz, you were allowed to own all kinds of pets so long as they were outside of the house. At different stages, I had rabbits, snakes (none poisonous, obviously), mice (white only, of course), bees (yes!), and dogs and cats. In short, it was a worry-free life—a true paradise.

At the age of six, on my first day at school, I entered the class and found my name on a desk in the second row. I was seated next to Mazal, a beautiful brunette with a ponytail, big hazel-brown eyes, and a stunning smile.

"Greetings, children," said our teacher, Bella. "Welcome to first grade."

She then asked us to open the drawers in our desks. In mine, I found a small chocolate bar; we each received one. I felt joy and happiness; it was a moment I will cherish forever. Then Teacher Bella pulled out a beautiful dark brown teardrop-shaped mandolin and played melodies from her childhood days in Minsk, Belarus. I was in love, though I'm not sure with whom, the astonishing six-year-old brunette seated next to me or with Teacher Bella, the mandolin wizard from Minsk.

At least once a week, Teacher Bella took us for a half-day trip out into the countryside around our kibbutz. To this day, Teacher Bella, a gentle old lady and a gifted musician, is my favorite teacher of all.

Growing up in Givat Brener, the biggest kibbutz in Israel, provided me with a unique opportunity I will treasure all my life; the opportunity to experience nature, to live with it at close hand through its annual cycle was a wonderful gift. I felt intoxicated by the perfume of the orange tree blossom and was devastated each year when it was washed away by mud floods and stormy winters. I felt reborn watching sprouts of wheat rise in brown fields and sad when they slowly dried out during months of drought before they'd had the chance to realize their full potential. My heart was filled with joy when Aunt Eta brought me the most adorable twins—white and brown pigeons—but I was heartbroken when they were slaughtered and eaten by a stray beast.

Introduction

Nature taught me that whatever is given to us does not really belong to us. We don't own it, so we had better appreciate it and enjoy it while it lasts.

When I was thirteen my family had to leave the kibbutz. My mom divorced my stepfather and we moved to live in Beer Sheva, "the capital of the Negev," a desert in the south of Israel. It was a devastating experience, but at the same time it forced me to cope with a tougher reality. For the first time in my life I felt scared and insecure. I had to meet new kids and I didn't know how they would treat me. Would I be able to make new friends? I felt helpless. On my very first day at school, I realized that kids are the same everywhere; they all share the same basic needs. All kids want to enjoy life, to connect with others, to explore their own feelings, to be inspired.

Soon enough, I accepted the new reality of life in the city. I learned how to use money, to cross roads only on a pedestrian crossing, and to wait until traffic lights turned green. No more living in paradise.

I made peace with myself and became great friends with other people. Beer Sheva was a melting pot of several nationalities and cultures. I was fascinated by the rich culture of our Indian neighbors. I warmed to the hospitality of my good friend Shalom's family that arrived from Tunisia. On weekends, Shalom and I would go to the Bedouin market on the outskirts of Beer Sheva, where the Bedouins traded camels and sheep. We would stroll among the antique traders and drink sweet, strong, freshly brewed black coffee from small cups. Walking in that magical place made me feel as if I was sailing to another planet.

During school vacations and holidays, I would travel back to the kibbutz, the only place where I could fully embrace nature, a place I felt inspired, where I felt at home, and where I could close my eyes and exhale.

When I became an adult I lived in Tel Aviv, with the Mediterranean as my natural refuge. Whether it was a misty winter dawn, or a hot steamy summer night, only on Gordon Beach, either sitting on the golden sand or floating on the sea, could I truly live and experience nature again. Even just a few snatched minutes revived me, at sunrise on my way to work or at sunset on my way back home.

Since I left Israel in 1993, I've been fortunate to have lived in several countries—USA, Cyprus, and for a short period, India—and I was fascinated by those cultures. Carrying the kibbutz bliss within me everywhere I went, I searched for that outer and inner paradise, whether it was the magnificent St. Louis, Missouri Forest Park, the charming pine forests on top of the Troodos Mountains in Cyprus, the wild magical jungle of Kerala in southern India, the holy Ganges in Varanasi, or the mystical Golden Temple at Amritsar, in northern India.

In all the places I've visited and in all cultures I have been exposed to, I couldn't help but notice that regardless of nationality or religion, we all, at some stage in our lives, pause to pay attention. Some hold their breath, some begin to wonder, others question their existence—why are we here? What is our purpose?

I was no exception. I had reached a certain stage of my life and felt that I was missing something I could not describe. I couldn't put my finger on it, but a restless feeling of being incomplete dominated my whole existence.

At the time, I was living in St. Louis. I was forty-five years old, I liked my job as a computer software engineer, and I had pretty much everything that a middle-class person wanted or needed. Still, there was a nagging emptiness within me. Then, in the winter of 1997, I heard about a weekend workshop on shamanism in New Orleans. That workshop—that weekend—changed my life completely.

After the workshop, I returned to St. Louis and slipped right back into my seventy-hour-week workaholic lifestyle and my familiar routine. But life was not meant to be routine for me. That shamanic workshop awakened a spiritual seed in me that began to sprout. It created a hunger in me for more. I longed for change and an alternative way to live my life. I practiced shamanic journeys, I studied Reiki and became a Reiki master, I studied Tai Chi. I went from meat-filled lunches and dinners to green salads. Organic foods appeared on my plate more and more often.

A little about shamanism. The word "shaman" derives from the Siberian Tungus people and means "the one who knows." It describes their healers and medicine people. The shaman makes a spiritual journey to three dimensions—Lower, Middle, and Upper Worlds— for healing purposes and to receive answers to questions. When practicing shamanic spiritual journeys you may meet your Power Animals, Spiritual Guides, and Teachers in one of those three worlds.

In the following chapters, I share my personal experience during that weekend in New Orleans, and the incredible journeys when I met Dolphin and Bear, my Power Animals, the amazing Hilla, my Spiritual Guide, and my Teacher Elijah the Prophet, who is the main reason I walk the path of shamanism.

My hope, dear reader, is that my words are not taken lightly. I am compelled to share with you this dramatic change in my life. It was an enormous shift from incompleteness to a sense of fulfillment and bliss.

In September 2001, I moved to the beautiful island of Cyprus, where I lived for four remarkable years. The first two years I lived in Amathus, a tiny pictorial village hanging on a cliff right above the deep blue Mediterranean. For the other two years there I rented a small, cozy home in the charming village of Saitas in the Troodos Mountains. Tall, lavish Pinus Nigra surrounded my house, black pines that generously shared their shade throughout the hot summer days, and provided warm shelter during cold winter nights.

Cyprus's natural beauty enhanced my willingness to share and give, and I started teaching Reiki on Sundays and Tai Chi on Thursday nights. I continued my own shamanic development and journeyed for those who quested or who asked for answers, clarity, and spiritual guidance. I performed these tasks for no charge, thus allowing me time to focus on giving and sharing. The more I shared, the more confident I felt that I was walking the right path for my own spiritual growth.

But life was not meant to be routine for me. That shamanic workshop awakened a spiritual seed in me that began to sprout. It created a hunger in me for more. I longed for change and an alternative way to live my life. I practiced shamanic journeys, I studied Reiki and became a Reiki master, I studied Tai Chi. I went from meat-filled lunches and dinners to green salads. Organic foods appeared on my plate more and more often.

Chapter One:

Are You My Teacher?

~~~ — ~~~

New Orleans was sunny on that warm winter day as we walked across the empty parking lot towards the charming New Age store. I felt excited, aware that I was facing the unknown, facing something that aroused my insatiable curiosity. Little did I suspect that the entire course of my life was about to change.

A few weeks earlier, on a cold, gloomy Sunday afternoon in St. Louis, a friend and I had been sitting at the Grind, a cozy coffee place in the Central West End. She was telling me about the anthropology classes she was taking at the Community College when suddenly she remembered something.

"Doobie, have you ever heard of shamanism?" she asked, picking up her coffee mug.

"No, I haven't," I said, frowning at her over my double espresso.

"I'm going to an Introduction to Shamanism workshop in New Orleans in about three weeks' time," she explained. "I'd love for you to come along. I'm sure you'd enjoy it. We could stay in a hotel and head back home on Sunday night."

I love going to New Orleans, mainly for its great fresh seafood.

"Okay," I said. "I'll go with you—on one condition. We have to have dinner at my favorite seafood place, The Pelican Club." I had been craving their fresh oysters, delicious shrimps and scallops in a lemon and butter sauce, finished off with steamed lobster.

"I take it that's a yes," she said, the lines creasing around her brown eyes as she smiled at me.

Three weeks later, I picked her up on Friday afternoon. As we drove south along the I-55, passing through Memphis, I turned to her and said, "By the way, what is shamanism? I don't even know how to spell it."

"I don't know," she said, taking me by surprise. Did she not know what we were getting into? "It was this little red leaflet here that sparked my interest." She pulled a piece of folded paper out of her coat pocket.

"Okay, I'll read it at the next rest area," I said.

As it turned out, the leaflet didn't reveal much. Its explanation went over my head, and I wasn't intrigued at all.

Traveling south to Louisiana was heaven. It was still winter there, but compared to freezing St. Louis, where you could see your breath coming out of your mouth, Louisiana was almost tropical. We headed to a New Age shop on the outskirts of New Orleans.

On Saturday morning, after a light breakfast at a nearby restaurant, we left for the workshop. After a short ride we parked in the vacant parking lot of a shopping center and walked towards the New Age shop, an old double-gallery house standing in the shade of a marvelous oak tree. The building had broad balconies across the front facade at both levels, supported by round, tall columns. Each level had wide

Chapter One

windows that looked like eyes, allowing lots of natural light into the house.

The door to the store was open. We walked across the wide wooden-planked floor and followed the sign towards the back of the store. Shelves there were packed with books. All kinds of Far Eastern meditation books filled the bookcase on the right-hand side, reaching up to the ceiling. Self-healing and healthy nutrition books were on the left-hand side, neatly organized on the bookcase adjacent to the wall. Soft sounds from a water fountain filled the air, along with the aroma of herbal tea that was brewing in a nicely designed oriental kettle standing on a small wooden table next to stairs that led up to the second floor. I saw packs of Tarot cards on a shelf under a window in the corner. Healing crystals and quartz placed in glass bowls were scattered around.

"Hi! Good morning," said a man with a deep voice. "Looking for the workshop?" His friendly smile flickered like we shared a secret. "My name is Ken. This is my wife Betty, and we own this shop."

"Good morning to you too," I said. "Yes, we're here for the Introduction to Shamanism workshop."

Right away we felt welcome and at home. Betty kindly served us freshly brewed black Himalayan tea and we sat on comfortably cushioned chairs around a table by the window, looking out at the street. It felt soothing.

Then Ken said, "Let's go up to the second floor and meet the group."

We climbed the narrow wooden stairs and entered a spacious room, which radiated warmth and coziness. About fifteen people were sitting in the room; most of them were women. Some sat on the floor and some leaned against the wall. The morning light came through half closed shades on the windows. I felt truly relaxed and comfortable.

A few people talked in low voices while others prepared their practice space with blankets, pillows, drums and rattles. I liked the atmosphere and sensed the anticipation of the unknown in the air. Looking back, I realize that I felt as if something very exciting was about to happen.

Dolphin, the Power Animal

A man walked to the front of the room. He wore comfortable cotton clothes. As he lowered himself to the floor, he placed a rattle decorated with colorful feathers by his right side, a big round drum in front of him, and several wooden animal icons—a bear, a fox, an eagle, and a dolphin—on a small native Indian blanket to his left. A dark covered notebook sat in his lap. I followed his moves. He shut his eyes and meditated for a while.

He opened his eyes and lit a small candle in front of him. He looked around the room as if reading our hearts and minds. I noticed that everyone was silent. Then he smiled and said, "Welcome to New Orleans, and welcome to this Introduction to Shamanism workshop. My name is Dana and I'll be your facilitator."

His eyes scanned the group. "Why don't we go around and introduce ourselves, share with the group why you are here, and what your expectations are."

I felt a little nervous. Some people said, "I want to practice shamanism. I want to help myself and I want to help others." Others said, "This isn't our first workshop, but we're a little confused after attending a previous workshop. We don't think we're doing it right."

Me? I had no clue what on earth they were talking about. My friend didn't know either; she had a blank stare that said, "Let's get out of here."

My turn. I looked around. They were all Americans. They had all come prepared with nice handmade colorful rugs with geometric symbols on them. Some brought native Indian blankets with images of animals and Indian totems. They had rattles and feathers. They all looked at me, and even the candle in front of Dana seemed to point at me, an Israeli, a relative newcomer to the country.

"My friend"—I pointed to my friend on my right—"brought me here and I'm really looking forward to a seafood dinner later at The Pelican Club where the fish melts in your mouth."

Everyone laughed and Dana moved on to the next person.

I sat on my timeworn plain dark blue yoga mat. Next to me, on a vivid orange and green striped rug, sat John, a kind, blue-eyed hippie from Mississippi who had a long gray ponytail lying down his back. He had been to Introduction to Shamanism workshops before but had not succeeded in his journey to the Lower World. In front of me, Louis and Alice were seated on a fluffy brown and yellow blanket with big smiles in their eyes. They were African-Americans from Baton Rouge, Louisiana. They had been practicing shamanism for quite some time, and this workshop was their gift to Matthew, their eighteen-year-old son who they'd brought along. On the other side of the room, sharing a colorful red and purple psychedelic rug, sat Rachel and Annabel, two friends from Panama City, Florida. It was their first time to experience shamanism too.

From that moment on, Dana had my undivided attention. I was fascinated. My mind was captivated with each word, and my pencil sped across the page like an ancient Persian scribe. After all, what could be more fun and exciting than spending a weekend morning chasing spirits in other worlds and feasting on great Creole cuisine at night?

I looked at the other faces. They all seemed focused on themselves, expecting to experience something out of the ordinary. The room was silent.

Dana told us about shamanism and how it has been practiced around the world in places such as Siberia, Peru, and Australia. I was intrigued by the way he described shamanism. It felt as if I had entered into a secret place, a place I had never visited before yet a place that made me feel at home. I had never felt like this before.

Dana's voice interrupted my thoughts: "In the next few minutes we will begin our journey to the Lower World, and there we will meet our Power Animal. Next, when the time is right, we will journey, still in the Lower World, to meet our Spiritual Guides."

He looked at us, we all sat still. No one spoke.

"To practice shamanism regularly one should first meet one's guides. They are always there in the other worlds for us. We just have to 'go' and meet them. The method is quite simple. We will lie down on the floor, and I will start beating my drum. You will journey to the sound of my drum." He demonstrated a drumming sound, a nice, soothing, monotone that resonated with the natural rhythm of breathing and the beating heart. This rhythm vibrated deeply in my body. It awakened a strange feeling inside me, something familiar, almost as if it connected to a hidden layer touched a long time ago, deep inside me.

Then Dana's voice became husky and low: "You will lie down with your eyes shut. When you hear the sound of the drum, we will begin. Visualize the Earth's surface and then look for an entry in the surface, something that suggests an opening in the Earth's surface. Once you find the opening, slip into it and travel down into the open space, down into the Lower World. There, you will journey until you run into an animal, any animal, small or big, on land or in the sea—a fox, a snake, a tiger, a bird, a whale. Ask this animal, 'Are you my Power Animal?' If the answer is 'yes'," Dana continued, "you will return exactly the way you entered. Open your eyes, and write down notes about this journey. Paper and pens are on the table. Do this quietly as others may still be journeying. For those who have not found their animal, keep traveling in the Lower World until you meet your Power Animal who awaits you. When you have returned, sit quietly and write down your thoughts and feelings. Describe your experience of your first shamanic journey." He paused. "That's all! That will conclude your first journey."

The room was silent. That strange feeling in me would not subside, and somehow I felt reconnected to deep-rooted childhood places still warm in my soul.

I lay down on my yoga mat, which felt hard, but I didn't mind. Calm yet somewhat excited, I covered my eyes and took a deep breath. I felt glued to the floor. Dana's drumbeats seemed soft, and then the sounds ascended, almost vaulting up into the ceiling. The drum's sound slowly penetrated me, its steady rhythm filling me until I felt at one with it. Then I found my opening to the Lower World.

I was above an ocean, looking down into the deep crystal-clear water, and I saw a reflection of myself in the clear emerald-green water, deep down at the bottom of the ocean. I saw myself standing at the edge of a small hole at the bottom of the ocean—evidently it was my opening to the Lower World.

Without further delay, I plunged through the hole on to a huge water slide that spiraled deeply into the Lower World. I was thrilled and enjoyed every moment. But the fun ride suddenly ended as I glided straight into a little round water pool, about thirty feet in diameter, that was set in a cave with a curved roof. I stood in the pool, water up to my waist, feeling a great sense of joyfulness mixed with curiosity. I was facing three small wooden doors mounted in the cave wall. The doors were Hobbit-sized, with arched tops that curved to fit the cave's shape. Each door had a small metal knob on its left. The middle door was wide open; the two closed doors were covered with dust, and mud was piled up in front of them. It looked as if those two doors had been closed for a long time.

Pale light was coming through the open door. I felt as if I was being pulled towards this light. I stepped out of the circular pool and walked through the open middle door towards the light. I couldn't see much but I continued to push myself forward, and as soon as the shadowy cave was behind me, I was amazed to see an ocean shore in front of me. The sand on which I stepped barefoot felt like silk. I walked slowly and, strangely, left no footprints. It felt as if my feet were cradled in love. Palm trees dotted the landscape and the emerald ocean glistened and sparkled.

I was filled with an increasing sense of astonishment as I stood on the edge of this dazzling ocean. Suddenly, a beautiful dolphin came towards me, its sleek gray back arching out of the water. The dolphin looked at me and smiled, happy to see me—yes, he actually smiled. I was stunned. My throat vibrated as a question from deep within me emerged.

"Are you my Power Animal?" I asked.

"Yes," he replied. "My name is Dolphin."

"Thank you," I said.

He raised his magnificent glistening body out of the water, shaking off droplets of water, and hovered upright, his tail just touching the surface. He leaned closer to me, and I could smell a salty water scent from his smooth skin. He looked into my eyes, smiled, turned his head to the water and then disappeared into the deep. It was a moment I will remember forever. I felt safe, free, and happy, and I did not want to leave that beautiful place. I had met my Power Animal, Dolphin.

Reluctantly, I turned to go back the same way I had come and arrived back in the room to find myself lying on the yoga mat on the hardwood floor. I was back in our dimension; Dana was still drumming.

I lay still on the floor, but my mind exploded, overcome by the amazing experience. What was that? I thought incredulously. What was that journey, that experience I just went through? I felt that if I tried to rationalize or explain it, it would ruin the whole experience. I opened my eyes. Only four minutes had passed. I raised my head and looked at the inert bodies lying next to me, still journeying. A while later, Dana accelerated the drumbeat, a signal for us all to finish our journeys. Then a couple minutes later, he stopped drumming.

One by one, everyone opened their eyes, sat up and began writing down notes. We were all still under the influence of our recent experience, but we slowly began to talk to each other.

"I met a beautiful wolf," someone said with great joy in her voice.

"I didn't succeed. I couldn't find an entrance to the Lower World," I heard another person say with great sadness.

Others sat with a serious expression on their faces and didn't speak at all. The soft sounds of conversation hovered like low cloud over the room. It felt strange to be there, in a place I had just come to know, with people I'd never met before, and yet we had all just shared a powerful spiritual experience. It felt odd, but it was also the first time I felt that I was doing something different, something exciting, something I would want to repeat.

I looked at Dana's closed eyes and the drum sitting next to him. Was he listening to the conversations in the room? As if I had spoken my thought out loud, he opened his eyes, surveyed the room, and waited for silence. He began to tell us more about the shamans, what they did for the tribe, for their people. Then he asked, "Who would like to share their journey with the group?"

Only two people volunteered. I was surprised to hear that quite a few participants hadn't been able to find their Lower World; they said they couldn't locate an opening in the Earth. I hesitated. Should I tell Dana and others about my journey? Should I share about Dolphin? When Dana asked again for a volunteer, I raised my hand. There was complete silence in the room when I told them in great detail about my journey. I was thrilled that I, Doobie Shemer, the kibbutznik from Kibbutz Givat Brener in Israel, was sitting in New Orleans humbly telling everyone in the room about how I had found my opening to the Lower World, and describing the water slide, the door in the cave, how I had met Dolphin, and how wonderful it was to journey.

~~~ — ~~~

Suddenly, a beautiful dolphin came towards me, its sleek gray back arching out of the water. The dolphin looked at me and smiled, happy to see me—yes, he actually smiled. I was stunned. My throat vibrated as a question from deep within me emerged.
"Are you my Power Animal?" I asked.
"Yes," he replied. "My name is Dolphin."
"Thank you," I said.

~~~ — ~~~

Hilla, the Spiritual Guide

After a short break, we reconvened and went back to our places on the floor. We lay down on our mats, some covered themselves with blankets, and we all closed our eyes ready for our next journey—back to the Lower World. This time, we were to meet our Spiritual Guide—a human spirit. A sense of excitement pulsated around the room. We all knew the question we were to ask: "Are you my Spiritual Guide?" If the answer was "yes," we were to come back and make notes. If the answer was "no," we were to continue our journey.

I couldn't wait. A heightened state of wonder wrapped around me like a soft white blanket. I instructed my body to be still, and my ears tuned in to the beat of Dana's drum. Whiteness blanketed me, and within seconds I was back at the bottom of the ocean. I entered the same hole, swam down the spiral slide towards the cave with three doors, and stepped out through the open door onto the beautiful beach. The sparkling ocean stretched towards the horizon and I was drawn to the vision of Dolphin cavorting along the shore.

I clearly remember there was no conversation, but there was a definite sense of knowingness and of interconnectedness. Calmness washed over me; it was the kind of feeling you want to last forever. It felt as if Dolphin and I had known each other for eternity.

I got up and I walked towards the palm trees to search for my Spiritual Guide. I looked at Dolphin, and as he read my silent call for help, he turned towards me and said, "Wait, she will soon be here."

I remained where I was, taking in the beach's unusually bright sand and the clear, pure seawater. I saw Dolphin's sleek curves as he arched and dove rapidly into the ocean. Suddenly, a blue aura emanated from behind me in the sand. What was that? I turned and looked more closely. Playing cards gradually appeared as if someone was dropping them into the sand. They stood up vertically in the white glossy sand a few inches from each other, row after row of them across the entire beach. I gasped and stared at them; I'd never seen, nor imagined, anything like this.

Each card was as tall as I was and about four feet wide, and depicted the image of a human face. On the card in front of me, I could clearly see an old man gazing to one side over my left shoulder. His long gray hair covered most of the card's surface. He was expressionless, but I could feel his presence; a strong sense of wisdom emanated from him. This was someone I could trust to guide me, to save me. I was stunned and I couldn't speak. I needed help.

Dolphin swam close to the edge of the shore. "Talk to them," he said.

I turned back to face the cards, preparing to question them. Then a woman stepped out of one of the cards and walked languidly towards me. She had long, silky straight jet-black hair and dark olive skin, and her long, dark brown dress clung to her slender body. She stopped a few steps in front of me, looked straight into my eyes, and waited for me to say something. It felt as if I had been waiting to meet her all my life, as if she was someone I needed in my life but hadn't known it until now. Her piercing black eyes transfixed me and I felt calm and peaceful.

"Are you my Spiritual Guide?" I eventually asked.

"Yes," she said and smiled. "My name is Hilla."

Chapter One

I was unable to move or talk; waves of humility washed over me.

"I am your Spiritual Guide," she continued. Her eyes, changing color to deep, soft shades of browns and greens, penetrated my very being.

I was filled with gentle energy, warmth, and love. Near Hilla's feet, half buried in the pure white sand, I saw three large rocks jutting out. The rock on the left was crimson, with tones of dark red through it; the middle rock was a deep blue color, like a summer sky; the third rock, on the right, was a vivid green, the color of fresh grass at dawn.

Nothing was ordinary, or normal, any more—red was no longer just red; blue and green were much more than that—these colors were other-dimensional. I felt a childlike urge to bend over and pick up one of the rocks.

"No need to pick them up," said Hilla softly.

I paused, surprised, and looked at her.

"You already have them. They are within you," she explained.

"Within me? What are they?" I asked.

"The blue rock is the healing stone, the green is the energy stone, and the red is the love stone," Hilla replied.

Then she turned and walked away from me; hypnotized, I watched her disappear from view into the forest of palm trees.

I wanted to stay; I didn't want this enlightening, breathtaking experience to end. But I knew my mission was over for now. So I turned to travel back to the room and awakened to find Dana still drumming. Again, everyone else appeared to be still journeying. I opened my eyes and gazed at the prone bodies.

In that moment, I knew my life would never be the same again. I lay there on the wooden floor of that New Age shop listening to shamanic drumbeats and the soft sounds of a New Orleans morning, and savoring the aroma of recently brewed tea, and I knew deep within my soul that something incredible had just happened. I knew it was a spiritual experience that I should not question, try to rationalize or justify. I also knew it was something I wanted to explore further and develop.

Gradually the other participants sat up and began writing notes. The drumbeats stopped, and Dana read a few paragraphs about shamanism from a brown, hardcover book, *The Way of the Shaman*. He explained to us what a shaman in a tribe would do to help the tribe to heal sickness, locate food, and even how to deal with rival tribes. He then asked if anyone would like to share their experience of their journey. This time, more people were open to sharing. I couldn't wait to tell everyone about meeting Hilla.

It was time to take a lunch break. We went down to the first floor where we had warm lentil soup and fresh bread, the tastiest lunch I had had for quite some time. There must be something about spiritual experiences that increases physical hunger. When I had finished my lunch I sat by a large window to process what had happened that morning. I felt elevated and happy in a way that I hadn't been for such a long time. I was eager to journey more, to experience more.

When lunchtime was over, we returned to the meditation room and sat in our places, ready for our next journey.

"Does anyone have a question?" Dana asked before we began.

John, the hippie from Mississippi, raised his hand. "May I comment?" he asked.

"Sure," replied Dana, smiling at him.

"I want to thank Doobie," John said. "I've been to two Introduction to Shamanism workshops before, but I've never managed to complete a single journey. Each time I started, I'd reach a well topped with dark blue water and I just stood next to it not knowing what to do." Then he looked at me, his eyes shining. I was surprised; I wasn't sure what to say. Then he looked back at Dana, and went on: "But after I heard Doobie's journey about the opening in the bottom of the ocean, I realized that I just have to dive into the well. So in my last journey, I dove into the water fearlessly, and for the first time, I managed to complete my journey to find my Power Animal, a beautiful Jaguar." John turned to me. "Thank you," he said.

I smiled at him. I could see the relief on his face. I felt humble, yet great joy and happiness filled my whole being.

"Thank you, John," said Dana. "And now it's time to journey to the Upper World. There you will meet your Spiritual Teacher. To cross to the Upper World you need to levitate above the Middle World. Eventually, you will feel a membrane. You need to pass through the membrane to the other side, to the Upper World. Once in the Upper World, you can begin your search, and once again you will ask those wondrous words, 'Are you my Spiritual Teacher?' If the answer is 'yes' then ask another question: 'Do you have a message for the group?' If the answer is 'No' then continue to search for your teacher."

Having found my Power Animal and my Spiritual Guide in the Lower World, I was excited and full of anticipation, but I was also uneasy about this Upper World journey to meet my teacher. How different would the experience be to the previous two journeys; how different would it be to meeting Dolphin and Hilla? Little did I know.

The drum throbbed and the beats penetrated my body deeply as Dana led us on our third journey. I felt soothed. I was ready.

"No need to pick them up," said Hilla softly.
I paused, surprised, and looked at her.
"You already have them. They are within you," she explained.
"Within me? What are they?" I asked.
"The blue rock is the healing stone, the green is the energy stone, and the red is the love stone," Hilla replied.

Elijah, the Teacher

I pushed myself up through a thick layer of cloud and landed on a soft, white cotton-like surface. Stillness prevailed. All I could hear was the sound of my own breathing. Slowly, I turned to look at my surroundings and found myself in the center of a vast white space. It seemed divine. I had a sense of no space and no time. I was enveloped by infinite whiteness, nothing but whiteness. "This is a heavenly never-melted snowfall," I thought.

Never in my life had I witnessed such glory and magnificence. The profound silence had a powerful presence; an amazing sense of power radiated from, and dominated, this dense silence. I stepped forward without any sense of direction or expectation. The word "Teacher" kept pounding in my heart.

The air around me felt very fresh, cool, and crisp. Suddenly, the shape of something tall appeared in front of me. As I continued to walk, the vision crystallized into the wall of a giant white palace, and I found myself standing in front of an immense, glowing white marble gate with twin doors. The gate was shut. To the left of the gate was a large white marble chair. As I got closer, I noticed to my amazement that the marble was alive. It didn't move exactly, but gently vibrated and shimmered, and inside this marble I saw white, misty, wafting clouds that looked solid to the touch.

This entire scene—the palace, the gate, and the chair—looked like a living ice sculpture created by a minimalist artist with a strong sense of the divine. The sculpture radiated power, and I became rooted and still. It felt as if I were in the most sacred place in the universe. Then I heard a voice.

"The King sits on this chair."

"What King?" I asked spontaneously.

"The Guardian King," answered the voice.

I didn't know to whom I was talking—I could see no one—but I had a strong sense of another entity nearby. I turned to the right, and there, indeed, I saw the vague outline of a human figure gradually approaching out of the misty whiteness. Someone was walking towards me through the closed giant gate.

First, I saw his face, and then I noticed the long white beard that covered most of his face. I was transfixed; I could barely breathe. The closer he got, the more details emerged. He was as tall as me and was dressed in a long white cotton gown. He stopped a few steps in front of me, his eyes closed; his face radiated eminence, divinity, glory. As we faced each other, a sensation of other worldliness ran through my entire body.

This person's presence electrified me. He radiated so much energy and such power, and yet he seemed clothed in calmness. I was shocked, as if I had been hit by lightning. For the first time I experienced the full meaning of "irat kavod," a Hebrew phrase that might translate loosely as "fearful respect": I was filled with immense respect for this man, yet felt deeply humble and just a little afraid. Never before had I experienced emotions such as this in the presence of another person.

Chapter One

He slowly raised his head, his long white hair gracefully framing his majestic face. He opened his eyes and looked straight into mine. He didn't move or say a word. I was completely mesmerized as he stood looking at me. It took me a while to regain my senses. The experience was too much to absorb and I felt overwhelmed. All I wanted was to get out of there, but I couldn't move.

After what seemed like forever, I somehow found the courage to speak. "Are you my teacher?" I asked.

"Yes, I am," he replied.

His presence was overpowering. His energy engulfed me. I wanted to leave, but I suddenly remembered that I had another question to ask him. "Do you have a message for the group?"

"Yes," he replied. "Tell them that there is heaven."

I felt relieved as I turned around to leave. But his trembling voice stopped me.

"And tell them that everyone has a guardian angel," he said.

I looked at him for a moment, and with what little presence of mind I had left, I thanked him.

Spellbound, I started to walk away and then it struck me—my Teacher was Elijah, the great Prophet, the same Elijah who had been taken up in a whirlwind by a chariot and horses of fire into heaven. He had lived on Mount Carmel in northern Israel.

This is how Elijah and I met for the first time. After that meeting, and every time I journey to meet Elijah, I experience that same powerful feeling again. I know I am standing in the presence of a higher power; this holy person shows me my real place in this world and in the universe.

In all our conversations, I ask Elijah questions that are related to our existence and our purpose in life. Some are philosophical while some are personal. Even though our talks are short and to the point, each one is interesting and utterly meaningful.

Elijah is not effusive. Words of timeless wisdom break from his lips. He doesn't contribute additional information unless I ask for it. With Elijah, I can choose the direction we walk and the depth of our discussion. Every conversation is entirely unpredictable. Most of the time, Elijah is very serious; I'm never able to predict his mood or reaction to my questions. Sometimes, he is impatient; at other times, he is cynical. Rarely does he smile. Whenever I need advice, he is there for me.

Most of my journeys are to the Lower World—to Dolphin and Hilla. I also journey for friends and family, at their request, to receive answers about jobs and other subjects. But when philosophical questions arise, I journey to the Upper World—to Elijah.

I have had many journeys to the Lower World, to Dolphin and to Hilla, and for some reason, there are some things I never ask them about. Sometimes they decide it would be better for Elijah to reply to my inquiries.

Walking with Elijah is neither about me nor about Elijah. Rather it is about us all, about our lives and our existence. We are all human beings knowing that we are here to live, but not knowing what was before us, or what will be after us. We are truly passionate in our quest to understand the meaning of our existence, to learn why we are here and to discover our purpose. I dedicate my journeys to finding the answers to all these questions just by walking with Elijah.

―――

This person's presence electrified me. He radiated so much energy and such power, and yet he seemed clothed in calmness. I was shocked, as if I had been hit by lightning. For the first time I experienced the full meaning of "irat kavod," a Hebrew phrase that might translate loosely as "fearful respect": I was filled with immense respect for this man, yet felt deeply humble and just a little afraid. Never before had I experienced emotions such as this in the presence of another person.

―――

"Yes," he replied. "Tell them that there is heaven."
I felt relieved as I turned around to leave. But his trembling voice stopped me.
"And tell them that everyone has a guardian angel," he said.

―――

Chapter Two:

What Else is Up There?

~~~ — ~~~

Bear, my other Power Animal

I slipped into the black opening at the bottom of the ocean and plunged down the water slide. A delightful joyous feeling filled me as I slid into the Lower World. I stepped outside the water pool and looked towards the cave. Again, only the middle door was open. But this time, when I stepped through the open arched door I entered a dark place; I knew that I hadn't reached the familiar ocean shore. Indeed, as soon as the shadow of the cave was behind me, I was astonished to find myself in a magical forest.

The trees were bizarrely shaped: all of them had three or more trunks connected to short horizontal naked branches, and each trunk, halfway to its top, was covered with thousands of leaves, the strangest leaves I have ever seen. They were beautiful shades of green, some light green, almost yellow, others were dark green. They all were as thin as needles and extremely long—more than fifty feet long. The ground was covered with flat light green grass. Under the trees, I noticed broad, purplish white-spotted mushrooms scattered across the ground. They had huge stems and their tops were shaped like upside-down trophies. Suddenly, pale yellow sunbeams broke through the forest canopy of needle-like leaves. I looked back down to the ground and noticed a giant white polar bear sitting next to the cave door basking in the dappled sunlight. He stared at me, his big, piercing dark eyes watching me as if he was measuring my steps and reading my thoughts. His eyes mesmerized me, and as I walked towards him, my heartbeat quickened.

He looked magnificent, majestic with his shaggy, shiny snow-white fur. As I walked towards him, the landscape around him suddenly disappeared. His presence was powerful, yet still and peaceful. I knew he was waiting for me; I felt no fear. I continued towards him until I stood a few steps in front of him. He didn't move, but continued to look at me. His dark eyes were vast pools of kindness and wisdom into which I wanted to jump and be forever immersed. I felt drawn to his magnetic presence and I didn't resist.

Have you ever had the feeling, when meeting someone new, that they were someone you've been longing to meet and that they were your long-lost best friend—someone you could trust unconditionally? That was how I felt right then as I looked into the dark gentle eyes of my huge amazing bear friend.

This was Bear, my other Power Animal, who waited for me right there until I needed him. I climbed effortlessly onto his glistening white back, grabbed hold of his shaggy fur, and he took me into a vast misty forest. From then on, Bear became my companion and my carrier; we soared and swooped over many lands, and explored many worlds together.

We arrived at the ocean beach. Hilla's absence was noticeable. I didn't know where she was, and I was flooded with sadness. I missed her. In the distance, I saw Dolphin swimming towards us, gliding through the ocean waves. When he reached the beach we hugged with joy, and I sat on the shore. I didn't have to explain why I was there; both Bear and Dolphin knew. I had a question—"What is up there, beyond the white layer?"—and they suggested that Elijah would be the best person to answer my question. So I sat on Bear's back and off we went.

Our flight seemed swift. We soared gracefully over the familiar surface of the White World back to the silent place of sacred stillness and potency. Dolphin appeared moments later, skimming the surface of the milky-white mist, and the three of us went together towards the white palace not saying a word out of respect for the deep silence.

The giant, shining, white marble gate was wide open this time, welcoming us into the palace. We passed through the gate and entered a garden. In front of us in the distance I saw the palace, a magnificent white building with seven identical tall white marble towers with pointed tops, the towers ranged equidistantly along the front of the building. Strangely, the palace didn't seem to have any doors or windows. The garden between the palace and the gate was almost empty. Just inside the gate to the left sat a wide table with benches on each side. Both table and benches were made of translucent white marble. Their tops were flat and their legs were beautifully sculpted. To the right, halfway to the palace, there was a small white marble shed. I saw no one, but I sensed a powerful presence and felt the energy flowing around us. I had no clue what it could be.

Then, an incredibly powerful force pulled my gaze away from the palace back to the white table. I sensed an imperial presence, someone magnificent. Elijah was sitting waiting for us on the stone bench that faced us. I could see nothing behind him; he was completely surrounded by white emptiness. He turned and gestured with his hand across the white table, inviting me to sit down. Humbled, I lowered my eyes and silently sat on the bench across from him. Bear and Dolphin remained behind me, respectfully aware of the moment. I looked into Elijah's eyes.

How can I describe those eyes? Their dark pupils were wells of knowingness, wisdom, and insight. He looked at me so intensely that I felt he had read my face, my body, my mind, my soul. A feeling of wonder crept into my mind. Would I ever get used to this magnificent, penetrating gaze of his? I could sense Bear's and Dolphin's hearts pulse behind me. Nothing moved around us; none of us moved. Nothing was said. I knew that Elijah would speak when the time was right.

Elijah's eyes seemed to emanate sunlight. He looked as if he had been created by a master sculptor, carved from the most exquisite white marble in the universe. No sound came from his mouth, but his tightly shut lips stretched in a smile. During my years of walking with Elijah, I've learned that I don't need to use my voice. Elijah can read my thoughts.

I looked back down to the ground and noticed a giant white polar bear sitting next to the cave door basking in the dappled sunlight. He stared at me, his big, piercing dark eyes watching me as if he was measuring my steps and reading my thoughts. His eyes mesmerized me, and as I walked towards him, my heartbeat quickened.

Yellow

Suddenly, orbs appeared out of the mist in the distance. They were coming towards us above our heads. They were orbs of light such as I had never seen before. Some were as large as planets, like those I'd seen in a planetarium. At first, the orbs were yellow, the color of daffodils in first bloom, then they merged into one big yellow cosmos that was filled with yellow shapes, like headless serpents, floating and intersecting with one another.

Puzzled, I looked at Elijah. No words were spoken but he "heard" my question, "What is this yellow cosmos?" He repeated my unspoken question and paused, closed his eyes, and seemed to go deep within himself in a search for the wisest way to answer. Finally, he answered.

"This White World, where we are now, is where all the souls reside. Every soul goes up to the White World after it leaves the Earth.

They come here to be with the other souls. The souls come here to reconnect with the souls they had been involved with while they were on Earth. They come to learn what they have accomplished and to determine what they need to work on the next time they travel to Earth. We are now in what you humans call heaven. All souls come here at first, and from here they go back down to Earth to join with a new human body for as long as that human is destined to live."

I looked around me; it wasn't what I'd imagined heaven would look like—endless whiteness! Nevertheless, the feelings and sensations I was experiencing could not have been more heavenly. It was all was so pure, so relaxing.

"What about the Yellow World?" I asked.

"New souls are created on the Yellow World. Also souls that need to recover, renew, and heal may come to the Yellow World. Once they recover, the souls come back to the White World or move to other planets." Elijah paused to let me digest what he had just said.

I could only sit there listening, trying to understand what I had just seen and heard. Elijah remained silent. He had not moved since we arrived. His white gown covered his body, as if protecting him from being touched, keeping him distant from everyone.

"Other planets?" I asked. "Which other planets?"

"This White World, where we are now, is where all the souls reside. Every soul goes up to the White World after it leaves the Earth. They come here to be with the other souls. The souls come here to reconnect with the souls they had been involved with while they were on Earth. They come to learn what they have accomplished and to determine what they need to work on the next time they travel to Earth. We are now in what you humans call heaven. All souls come here at first, and from here they go back down to Earth to join with a new human body for as long as that human is destined to live."

Blue, Green, Red

Elijah didn't say a word. The Yellow World disappeared and was replaced by the image of a Blue World. This Blue World didn't seem as well defined as the Yellow World, yet it was also possessed of the same serpent-like figures, in different shades of blue, floating and intersecting with each other. It felt like a tremendous movement of energy, energy in all shades of blue—from turquoise to deep ultramarine—surrounding me and emanating a kindly presence.

Suddenly, the blue turned to green, and a whole new Green World appeared before my eyes. This new cosmos contained the shapes of headless serpents writhing inside, just like the yellow and blue cosmos, only they were in different shades of green. A few minutes passed and the Green World changed to red. This red was intense and overpowering, like the hot lava that spits from an erupting volcano, and again there was the same serpent-like pattern, but now in shades of red.

Throughout the entire time, I was rooted to the spot, fascinated by the magnificent visions—and then it hit me! These were the same colors as the three rocks in the white sandy beach where I met Hilla for the first time. She had told me that the red stone was love, the green was energy, and the blue was healing. I remembered reaching out to pick them up, and she told me there was no need; 'You already have them. They are within you," she had said.

But was I right in thinking there was a connection between those colored stones and these three colored cosmos? And if there was a connection, then why? I wasn't quite sure. This colorful introduction to the Yellow World and the other three was Elijah's way of explaining things to me—of communicating by visualization rather than by talking. I knew additional details would follow.

"Did you see it?" asked Elijah, his familiar deep, vibrant voice coming from the other side of the big white table.

"Yes," I replied. "I saw the blue, green, and Red Worlds. What are they?"

"Blue is the healing planet. Green is the planet of energy. Red is the planet of love, the planet of the Creator. Each planet provides a different source and wellspring for an individual soul's needs. The soul connects with these three colored realms while on Earth and while here, in the White World," Elijah explained. "When a soul resides in the human body, it keeps connecting to those three planets through the body's energy centers—what you refer to as chakras. The role of these energy centers is twofold. Firstly, they connect souls to the three planets, red, green, and blue. Secondly, they enable the physical body and soul to integrate and function fully together."

It made sense, and I wasn't surprised. I immediately felt as if I had gained a fuller picture—maybe the entire picture. We are body, mind, and spirit, and none of these aspects of ourselves function entirely alone; each has an effect upon the other. The soul is the channel between the chakras to the corresponding planet. The Root Chakra connects to the Red World, the source of love, which connects to the Creator. The Heart Chakra connects to the Green World, the source of energy, and the Throat Chakra connects to the Blue World, where healing takes place.

"Love is the most powerful energy; no soul can exist without it, either on Earth or in the White World," said Elijah, raising his voice to emphasize the importance of what he was saying. "Love comes from the Red World, from the Creator himself. It is the source of creation for humanity on both physical and spiritual levels. In its turn, the energy of the Green World is what makes all nature evolve and keeps it connected to the source. Once created by love, the energy keeps it alive."

I looked around and, in the distance, took in the entire white palace with its towers. It was so peaceful, this profound silence all around us. If this is where the souls are, how come I don't see any? I wondered.

Elijah continued talking.

"Healing with its blue color is what allows all life to heal, regenerate, and renew. Once living things are created by the red, energized by the green and healed by the blue, they are able to accomplish their purpose. Each one of the body's chakras is a micro-planet that exists within the body as long as the soul is present. There are more than three chakras. The other chakras' role is similar to the three main ones, the red, the green, and the blue; their color is a mix of those three main ones, as is their role. While in the White World, the souls are healed and energized by connecting directly with the appropriate colored World. In the White World, a soul recovers and assimilates lessons learned from living on Earth by connecting to the green and Blue Worlds. When a soul has been badly wounded or traumatized and requires major recovery, it connects to love, to the Red World."

I felt Elijah's words drill into the very marrow of my soul. He raised his head and looked deep into my eyes. I sensed that he was connecting to something I didn't know existed in me. A shiver ran along my spine. As with all my other walks with Elijah, I was amazed and overwhelmed by the unexpected information I learned. I wanted to hear more, but I sensed that this particular journey was over.

"Thank you," I finally managed to whisper.

Elijah's eyes penetrated my soul as if he was measuring my ability to deal with the magnitude of the perceptions and facts he had revealed to me. I raised my head and looked around. I could see hardly anything in the white foggy garden, yet it felt so peaceful. Bear and Dolphin were still behind me, silently waiting for the journey to end. I turned back to Elijah. His eyes were closed and his face was expressionless. I got up and backed away, keeping my eyes fixed on him until I joined Bear and Dolphin. Together, we returned to the gate. At the gate, I stopped and looked back. Elijah had disappeared. The white marble table glowed in its profound emptiness.

~~~ — ~~~

"Blue is the healing planet. Green is the planet of energy. Red is the planet of love, the planet of the Creator. Each planet provides a different source and wellspring for an individual soul's needs. The soul connects with these three colored realms while on Earth and while here, in the White World," Elijah explained. *"When a soul resides in the human body, it keeps connecting to those three planets through the body's energy centers—what you refer to as chakras. The role of these energy centers is twofold. Firstly, they connect souls to the three planets, red, green, and blue. Secondly, they enable the physical body and soul to integrate and function fully together."*

~~~ — ~~~

Chapter Three:

A Life Journey

We are born; we live our lives; we die young; we die in middle age; we die in old age. This knowledge rests within us—in our cells and in our hearts. We embrace this innate knowledge, but we don't talk about dying, do we? Yet there are so many unanswered questions. What is the nature of the human being? What is the nature of the human form? Why does it happen this way? What was the Creator's intention in designing this form? Why does existence materialize this way—birth, life, and death? In other words, what is the purpose of our physical reality?

Grandma Tova

I ask these questions with a collective universal awareness that runs like a thread through current and previous generations. The

Holocaust imprinted itself upon my genetic code. Haim, my dad, and his mother, Tova, were the only two from their family of seven children to survive the Nazi Holocaust. They both escaped the Nazi concentration camps to Israel. A couple of years later they came to live in Tel Aviv. In the summer of 1950, Haim was a tall, charming young man with blue eyes, and he fell in love with Elizabeth, a beautiful green-eyed blonde who was a young refugee from Belgrade, Yugoslavia. They married, and a year later my brother Arye was born. I didn't have to wait too long; I was born a year later, in July 1952.

When I was three months old, my dad died, leaving behind a devastated young wife, my brother, and me. His death traumatized his mother, my Grandma Tova. Grandma was born in Latvia. She was six feet tall and her skin was always sun-tanned. Her eyes constantly reflected endless kindness yet deep sadness. She worked hard in a bakery next to the old central bus station in Tel Aviv. During my childhood, we lived in Kibbutz Givat Brener. Each month, Grandma Tova would come to visit and bring us a batch of pastries, recently baked—delicious cones filled with fresh white cream. I remember how my brother and I would wait by 'the Iegul" (the circle), the only bus station, on Friday afternoons around 3pm, looking for her face in the bus windows. How sad we were when the last person got off the bus, and we'd realize she wasn't coming that Friday. But on other Fridays when she did come, we were so excited to see her. She would come down the steps carefully and smile at us. Not wanting to waste any time, we shamelessly pulled the delicious cream-filled cones out of her bag. Grandma Tova never disappointed us.

Later, our family came to live in Tel Aviv, and as a teenager, I visited Grandma Tova in her two-bedroom apartment. We would sit side by side on her balcony on Friday afternoons, where she prepared very sweet, hot black tea. Then we would read the weekend newspapers. Grandma Tova would read the Yiddish newspaper and I would read the Hebrew newspaper, *Maariv*. After a while, she would say "Achshav kushat," a mix of Hebrew and Russian, which means "now eat," and I knew it was time for her mouthwatering, heartwarming chicken soup with matzo balls. I thought it the nectar of the Gods!

Chapter Three

Grandma Tova spoke only Russian and Yiddish, and could only speak broken Hebrew. I spoke only Hebrew, so she gestured a lot with her large work-worn hands. Despite our language difficulties, she read my heart and I read hers. Stories spilled out of Grandma Tova about how she and Haim, my dad, managed to escape the Nazis. Her voice was sometimes deeply sad and weary; at other times she sounded proud. Then her hand would reach into her housecoat pocket and pull out an old black and white photo that was curled and yellow at the edges. She'd hold this photo as if she were holding a sacred object and murmur, "Haim! Oh Haim!" and then she would cry. I knew she loved my dad; she missed him terribly.

Then I became a young man and got married myself. My wife and I lived in Kiryat Menachem, a quiet, cozy suburb nestled on top of a hill surrounding Jerusalem. On bright nights, I could see the sparkling lights of Holy Old Jerusalem. Every couple of months, Grandma Tova would heft two big plastic green baskets brimming over with freshly picked vegetables and fruit she had acquired at the crack of dawn at Shuk Ha'Carmel, a farmer's market in Tel Aviv. She would poke at fruit, feel the weight of squashes, and haggle. Once she was satisfied with her booty, she would wait at a nearby bus station, stride up the bus steps, and settle in with her two baskets loaded with food for us. That journey from Tel Aviv to Jerusalem, a two-hour winding bus ride along the roads of Sha'ar HaGai and Mevaseret Zion, was not easy, even for someone much younger than Grandma Tova. She was over seventy and still tall; I still had to look up at her. I thought she was the strongest woman in the world.

One day shortly after Grandma Tova arrived and we had sat down to eat the delicious chicken soup she'd cooked in our kitchen, I said, "Grandma Tova, we are expecting a baby."

Her mouth opened and her green eyes were like saucers. With a hand to her heart and tears rolling down her cheeks, she whispered, "If it's a boy, please name him after my son, your father. Please call him Haim."

But as fate would have it, a few months later our daughter Shiri was born. A year later, Grandma Tova, by that time in her late seventies and still shopping at the Shuk Ha'Carmel, took the two-hour bus ride to Jerusalem with two green plastic baskets of vegetables and fruit to visit us. She stepped into our Jerusalem apartment and we exchanged greetings, she in her broken Hebrew mixed with Yiddish, and me with what looked like a new sign language.

"Grandma Tova, we have a surprise for you," I said. "Perhaps a baby Haim will come into our lives. We are expecting another child!"

Her eyes filled with tears. "You remembered," she said.

"How could I not remember?" I replied. 'Haim, your son, was my father."

A few months later our son was born. I telephoned Grandma Tova. I had barely greeted her before I burst out, "We have a son and his name is Haim." I loved Grandma Tova; she was so kind, so lonely, and we couldn't refuse her request.

Her voice cracked and I suspect tears fell from her beautiful eyes. She thanked me and promised to visit us in a week. Sure enough, exactly a week later she knocked on our door. I had never seen her so happy. Her face glowed and she even looked taller than usual. She stayed with us for a few days, helping with cooking and cleaning, and played a little with Shiri before she left.

With two small children, my wife and I were caught in a vortex, stuck in of a whirl of diapers, getting up during the night, feeding the babies. Time seemed to escape us. A few months passed and one evening the phone rang. I answered it.

'Is that Mr. Doobie Shemer?" asked an unfamiliar man's voice.

I felt my ribs contract.

The man continued in an officious manner: "Your Grandmother Tova wanted me to call you. She has not been feeling well, and is now at the Beth Israel hospital in Tel Aviv. She wants to see you."

Early next morning I drove to Tel Aviv. I was worried because Grandma Tova was never sick. Something was very wrong, I thought. I took the elevator to the third floor. Her room was right next to the entrance and I went in. A strong smell of medicines permeated the air. She was lying in bed under a large window. A lunch plate piled with untouched food stood on her nightstand.

I didn't recognize her. She lay between the white sheets looking like a little child lost in a mirage of white desert sand. Her eyes were shut, her skin pale; there was no light in the face that rested, expressionless, on the large white pillow. This isn't Grandma Tova,

Chapter Three

I thought. There must be a mistake! What had happened to the strong, six-foot-tall woman with tanned skin?

I felt a layer of sadness grow over my heart. Somehow, I knew she was dying. I walked to the side of her bed and held her hand, so frail and so weak. I kissed her forehead. I just couldn't let go of her hand. Then she slowly opened her eyes, and when she saw me her eyes filled with love; she smiled.

"What's wrong, Grandma?" I asked, a dull ache gripping my stomach. "Why are you here?"

"I am finished," she whispered in her broken Hebrew and Yiddish. "No live anymore." She closed her eyes. "Haim?" she asked.

"He's doing great," I reassured her. For a moment, I thought I saw her smile. I felt so helpless as I stood there looking at her.

I went to the nurse's room to ask about my grandmother. The nurse asked me to follow her back to Grandma Tova's bed.

"Please tell your grandma that she must eat. She has been here for a few days and refuses to eat anything," the nurse said sternly.

I looked at Grandma Tova. She found the strength to wave her hand and mumbled something that sounded like, "Pay no attention to that yapping nurse."

Then the nurse turned to me and asked, "Who is Haim?"

"My son," I said. "He was born just three months ago. Haim is also the name of my father, her son. He died a long time ago. But why are you asking?"

"Well," said the nurse, "your grandma keeps saying, 'Haim is back. I can leave now.'"

I was shocked. Never before had I felt so much regret that Grandma Tova and I couldn't speak the same language. I pulled a small wooden chair up and sat beside her bed, gently taking her hand in mine.

"Grandma, I understand," I whispered. "You decided to end your life, now that my son Haim is born, right?"

She opened her eyes, looked at me, and smiled with a tired, yet peaceful smile. There was acceptance and peace in her eyes as she gently nodded her head.

Grandma Tova passed away a few weeks later.

Dying and Beyond

One afternoon in winter, a light snow started to fall as my flight landed at Ronald Reagan National Airport in Washington D.C. A few minutes later I drove a rental car towards the Pine Tree Lodge for a weekend workshop on Dying and Beyond, an advanced shamanic workshop.

Since the Introduction to Shamanism workshop in New Orleans, I had become good friends with Dana, the workshop facilitator, and I'd received an invitation from him to attend Shamanic Dying and Beyond. I remembered that introductory shamanism workshop in New Orleans well, and I was eager to expand my shamanic practice. This one was all the more enticing since Dana was the facilitator, and I was really looking forward to this workshop.

The ride was smooth along the country roads covered in a beautiful white lacework of snow. I felt peaceful and happy, and later that day I pulled into the Lodge's parking lot, savoring the sounds of the snow crunching under the car tires. It was twilight. I got out of the car and turned towards the sinking sun, its fading light filigreed through the clouds, and falling on the dark green pine trees. I soaked up the sheer beauty and divinity of the natural world that surrounded me, taking deep lungful of crisp, cold air and enjoying the crunch of snow under my feet. I felt calmness washing over me.

I went into the main cabin, a large room with a dark wooden floor. To the right was a red brick fireplace. The wall opposite was packed from floor to ceiling with books and magazines. A few people sat on a large dark red sofa and chairs. To my left was a door leading to the kitchen. I could smell something cooking. The fire had been lit, and the sweet smell of burning pine needles filled the cabin. I introduced myself to the others, some of whom I had met before, and then Dana came in. We hugged; it had been a long time since we'd last met. We were all excited to learn more about shamanism and to practice more. We had dinner in a restaurant not far away and then returned to our lodge to sleep in the main cabin.

Morning arrived and right after breakfast our workshop started. I didn't know what to expect; I was just eager to learn as much as I could about dying, death, and the afterlife from a shamanic perspective.

Chapter Three

We rearranged the living room so we would have enough space on the wooden floor to spread out our blankets and rugs, and to arrange our rattles, animal totems, and other shamanic tools that we'd brought. It was mid morning and it had stopped snowing; the sun was bright in the sky. The morning seemed magical. Snow blanketed the pine trees, the branches bowing towards the ground under its weight, and splashes of sunlight broke through the patchy clouds.

Dana, wearing a brown sweater and soft moleskin green pants, stretched his legs and smiled gently as he glanced around at the participants. He opened the workshop by blessing us all and asking us to introduce ourselves. There were fifteen people there altogether from various cities across the East Coast, and after a short introduction Dana briefly described the shamanic approach to dying and the afterlife.

"Participants learn ways of dealing with the issue of dying and the destiny of souls from a shamanic perspective," he explained. "This workshop will be helpful for those who wish to practice shamanism for themselves and for those who wish to help others who are perhaps terminally ill. Finally, some of you may find yourselves reconnecting with those who have gone, who have already passed on. In this weekend workshop you'll learn how to become experientially familiar with after-death realms. You'll learn how to use shamanic journeys to help people complete unfinished business and cross over. We'll also learn how to conduct psychopomp work—guiding a soul to the afterlife, or through the moment of death. A psychopomp also has the ability to search for lost souls, find them, and guide them home."

Our first journey was to meet one of our relatives who had passed away, Dana told us, and went on to instruct us how.

"Think of a relative that you'd like to meet. Ask if you can help him or her. I will beat my drum as you all journey to the Lower World to meet your Power Animals. Your Power Animals will aid you in meeting your relative. Once you find them, ask if he or she needs help, and if so, what kind of help. Sometimes all they need is just to be able to talk about something unfinished. But sometimes their soul is trapped on Earth and they need help moving on to another realm. All you have to do is ask."

One winter morning in October 1952, my dad was found dead. I was just a baby when he had been shot in cold blood several times in the chest and left to bleed to death on the beach at Jaffa in Tel Aviv. At the workshop, I was immediately consumed by an intense desire to meet him. I felt I was ready for our rejoining. I wanted to talk to him so much, but I was also anxious at the thought of it and felt a tightening in my chest, even though I knew I was in a safe environment. The people around me seemed to be experiencing similar emotions. But Dana would take care of us all.

I stretched out on my blanket, covered my eyes, and took a deep breath. The silence in the room seemed loud. A dog barked in the distance, and the burning pine logs in the fireplace crackled. These were warm, reassuring sounds.

Dana's drumbeat began with a gentle but rapid tap. The soft tones of the drum were feathery to begin with and then became firmer and stronger. Instantly, I dove down to the Lower World to meet my guides, my spirit helpers. Bear was waiting for me at the magical forest, bathing in a pool of sunlight that had broken through the thick canopy of long, needle-thin dark green leaves. Bear gazed straight at me—his dark eyes were pools of kindness and wisdom—and I realized he knew what my mission was. He knew I wanted to meet my dad. I climbed effortlessly onto his glistening snow-white back, and once I had a firm grip of his fur, we flew up in the air. Bear was carrying me to meet my dad and to new revelations ahead.

"Once you find them, ask if he or she needs help, and if so, what kind of help. Sometimes all they need is just to be able to talk about something unfinished. But sometimes their soul is trapped on Earth and they need help moving on to another realm. All you have to do is ask."

Chapter Three

Dad

We landed on a stretch of seashore I didn't recognize. It was dark; only the pale light of the moon shone on the waves that washed the white sandy shore. I looked around and suddenly saw a face; I knew it was he. He looked exactly like he did in his photos, as if time had stopped when he died. My dad was a young man in his mid twenties, with fair skin and dark hair; he was tall and extremely handsome. He smiled at me, but his eyes reflected deep pain. I could see that he had suffered—was still suffering—and I felt his pain. He stood only a few steps away from me but all I could really see was his face. I stepped closer to him and immense sadness enveloped me.

"Dad?" I said.

He didn't say a word, just continued to smile at me despite being in obvious pain.

"Why?" I asked. "Why did you die? Why did you go away?"

His eyes dilated in pain and his body became covered with blood. He looked weak and frail. I wanted to touch him, but I felt paralyzed. So I just stood there. Bear lay down on the sand a few feet behind me, my personal protector. Only the sound of the waves rushing to the shore broke the dark night's silence.

"So I would not interfere with your life, with your development, with you making progress in your life," he said after a while.

I was stunned. "Can I help you, Dad?" I eventually asked. "Should I carry you to a better place?"

"Yes please, son. Would you please?" he replied, almost whispering.

I held out my arms to enfold his wounded body and helped him to climb onto Bear; I sat behind him. Bear stood up carefully and then flew into a vortex of light, up and away from that dark beach where my dad had been trapped for so long. We flew directly to the Upper World, to the White World where he would be surrounded by love, where he could recover, and where I could come to visit him.

We entered the white garden through the open gate and got off Bear. Dad stood by me and rested his hand on my left shoulder. I studied his face. Gone was any trace of pain or agony; his eyes radiated kindness and calmness; there was no sign of blood on him. I was amazed by this transformation. He appeared washed with love, and it seemed as if an instantaneous healing had occurred. His miseries had evaporated.

"Thank you, my son," he said looking straight into my eyes. When he smiled it was pure and serene. "You may return to your life now, but please come back so we may meet again."

"Yes, Dad," I replied. I felt enormous joy. I had got my dad back, and from now on I could talk to him at any time.

―――

*"So I would not interfere with your life, with your development, with you making progress in your life," he said after a while.
I was stunned. "Can I help you, Dad?" I eventually asked.
"Should I carry you to a better place?"*

―――

"Your Son is Your Father"

Our next journey was to meet our Spiritual Guide to ask, "Is there anything you would like to share with me about a relative, either living or deceased?" Though death is not an easy subject to deal with, this isolated lodge covered in snow in rural Maryland seemed to be the perfect place for this discussion.

We all lay down once more on the wooden floor, covered our eyes, and to Dana's drumming rhythm we started the journey. I decided to visit Elijah, so I went straight up to the White World this time.

I arrived in front of the open gate. The sight of the spectacular white palace never failed to amaze me. The whole garden was vibrant in its whiteness, and I almost felt its living essence. I didn't see anyone, but I sensed that the garden was full of vitality. It felt as if it was constantly in motion that nothing was still. I knew a lot had happened in this garden, and yet I couldn't see anything. Perhaps I was not allowed to see just yet.

I went into the garden where Elijah appeared to be standing next to the big white marble table. His hands, crossed on his chest, were covered with the long white sleeves of his gown. As I walked

Chapter Three

towards him, he turned, raised his right hand, and signaled me to go with him farther into the garden. I felt pulled by a hidden magnetic force as I followed his footsteps, and as we walked, I could feel that serene yet powerful energy around us.

Then Elijah stopped, stepped into a small circle of pale light on the ground to his right, and started floating forward towards the palace, as if he was carried on an invisible stream. Amazed, I followed him. I stood in the same circle of light and floated alone. The stream took us deep into the magical garden, a place I had never been before. We floated straight towards the palace and Elijah stopped next to the tower on the far right. It seemed to point to the sky, as if in earnest prayer. Elijah looked back at me and motioned me inside.

But there aren't any doors, I thought. Nor are there any windows. How are we to get in?

Elijah answered my question by just stepping through the wall of the tower and continuing to walk. Why not give it a try? I thought, and I stepped in right after him, although I was in a daze and a state of complete disbelief—we had just passed through the wall as if it wasn't there! I was amazed and extremely curious. Where was Elijah leading me to exactly, and for what reason?

We were now inside the white palace. It was a glorious white structure, suggesting something celestial and heavenly. I had a sense of the divine, but really, my poor mind couldn't take it all in.

Elijah suddenly stopped at a small courtyard where three benches were arranged in a rough circle. No one else was there except Elijah and I. He sat on a bench and ordered me to sit next to him. He raised his left hand, and as he did so, I saw a person approaching us from the other side of the courtyard. My heart thumped in my chest—it was my dad! I was speechless. My dad sat on the remaining bench facing us. No one spoke.

I looked back at Elijah in amazement. He kept his eyes shut.

"You are here to ask me about your son," Elijah said, his voice like deep rolling thunder.

A shiver coursed through my entire body.

"Yes," I replied, only then realizing that that was what I had come for—to speak about my son Haim.

"But what about him?" I asked. "Why are we here? And why is my dad here?"

Elijah didn't respond straight away, but then I felt his hand clutch mine and when he spoke, his voice echoed through to my soul.

"The life journeys of humans are not random," he said. His mouth hadn't moved; his face was expressionless; his eyes were still shut.

"The goal of a life journey is to help build up a soul, to give it a path on which it can learn, grow, develop, and mature. A single physical lifetime is rarely enough time in which to achieve this; it may take several lifetimes. A soul usually has to go through a few life cycles before it can realize its true purpose."

Elijah paused. I felt that he was challenging me, trying to discern my ability to take in and digest what he was saying.

"Every soul on Earth, while in a human body, has a purpose—sometimes more than one," he continued. "Once these objectives have been accomplished, the soul then leaves the human body on Earth. In your world, this departure is referred to as dying. In order for a soul to develop, the Creator has given it instruments to work with—the mind and the body, and a path on which to travel—the stages of a life cycle. Shortly after the moment of conception is when the soul enters the human body. During the body-forming stage, the soul adjusts itself to function within its bodily limitations. Later, after the baby enters into this fleshly matrix, when it is still physically dependent, the soul still carries a memory of previous life experiences and reaches out to other souls in the baby's environment, laying the groundwork for its life ahead and establishing the course of its progress. This is a critical stage for the infant and, therefore, critical for the soul too. Just as the body is sensitive to neighboring hazards, so is the soul. The baby is still new to this dimension and can easily get hurt. Sometimes, the soul can experience trauma so intense that it gives up and leaves the body. Then the baby dies."

Elijah was silent for a moment. It felt as if he was giving me a chance to process what I just heard. I looked at him sitting there, his eyes still closed. I felt his warm soothing energy flowing towards me. My dad had said nothing; he had a serious expression on his face and a sense of calmness radiated from him.

"Is that one reason why babies die?" I asked. "Because the soul couldn't cope—because it was suffering?"

Elijah didn't answer immediately; then he said, "Yes, sometimes. Sometimes it's the physical body that can't overcome the obstacles or can't be healed. In other cases, it's because the soul gives up and decides to leave this life's journey. At other times the baby's soul has accomplished its purpose and so leaves, and sometimes, it leaves Earth altogether in order not to hurt other souls or interfere with other souls' development. When a soul is ready to come to Earth, it knows what it needs to accomplish and with whom. It works to achieve its purpose. It chooses the human body and his or her parents appropriate to the lessons or tasks ahead. Then while it's at the baby stage, the soul needs to determine how it will achieve its purpose. Sometimes it just can't figure it out, and sometimes it gives up because the other souls it was supposed to work with have left. The soul knows it will have to return, but it prefers to return to Earth when it is better prepared or equipped to accomplish its tasks and to learn its lessons. There are also times when a soul remains on Earth only because it needs to help other souls. For example, parents' souls have a purpose to achieve or a lesson to learn with the help of their baby's soul. In such cases, the baby's soul's only purpose is to help its parents' souls to progress; once it has done this, sometimes only a few months after the baby is born, its soul leaves Earth and the baby dies."

As often happened when I journeyed to visit Elijah, I wasn't quite ready for that level of teaching and insight. I was there to listen though, and I knew I would share this information with others some day.

"This is where the life journey of a soul starts," continued Elijah after a short pause. After the baby stage, a soul most likely knows how it will develop itself so it can learn its lessons and achieve its goals. As the human matures and becomes more independent, the soul is given additional skills and tools to help it to progress and learn. Then, during the stage of childhood, as the body develops, so does the soul. The soul works with other souls in order to accomplish its tasks. It's rare that a soul does not need interaction with, or support from, other souls. That is the stage when real learning begins, and when the soul gains more confidence in itself and its ability to accomplish its goals."

Thoughts raced through my mind. Could the soul's childhood stage be equivalent to the school period of our lives? After all, both childhood and school make us ready for adulthood and independence.

"Right," Elijah said, as if reading my mind. "At the childhood stage the soul learns all about what it needs to accomplish, and once the body functions independently, the soul starts to implement whatever it has learned." He paused. "A soul doesn't always succeed though. Not all souls manage to accomplish everything they should accomplish. Sometimes, it repeats wrongdoings it made in a previous life. In order to succeed, sometimes a soul has to overcome obstacles that are the result of conflict with other souls and their goals, or of a soul having its own mind."

"Then how can a soul make sure it accomplishes its purpose?" I asked.

"All human life cycles are similar. The soul and what it needs to accomplish are what makes the difference. For the soul to succeed, it has to maintain a connection with the angels and the Creator. This is what ties the soul to all the resources it needs—energy, healing, love—while it continues its presence on Earth in the human body."

"Are men and women different when it comes to souls?" I asked.

"A soul has no preference for the gender of human it travels with. A soul can be in a man's body for one life journey, and the next time it may come back in a woman's body. It depends on what it needs to accomplish in a life journey and with whom. The soul will decide which gender is more suitable once it knows what purpose it has to accomplish and right before it emerges into a baby's body."

"Does the soul's growth correlate to physical age?" I asked.

"No," said Elijah. "A soul does not relate to any physical age. A soul's growth comes with accomplishments, but the soul needs a human mind and body in order to progress. That is why the Creator created life on Earth in the form of cycles. The cycles allow souls to develop, to progress in parallel to the physical body, from the time they are born to the day they die—throughout a whole lifetime journey. And within a lifetime cycle lies the cycle of day and night.

At night it is the soul that dominates the course of one's development, while during the daytime, the mind dominates."

"At night?" I repeated, looking at Elijah. "How?"

"Through dreams," replied Elijah. He leaned forward as if he was trying to get my full attention. "Dreams are one of the ways that the Creator guides the soul and helps one's development throughout a lifetime," he continued. "In dreams, the soul channels the information needed for the person to make progress and accomplish their purpose. But it's up to the person's mind, when they're awake, to decide how this information is to be used and when action needs to be taken."

Elijah paused again, giving me time to collect my thoughts. There were quite few stories about people in many fields—science, art, and technology—who had received life-changing information, ideas, and answers in their dreams. Paul McCartney, for example, dreamt the tune of the song "Yesterday," which some claim is one of the Beatles' best songs. Otto Loewi won the Nobel Prize after he dreamt of an experiment to prove his hypothesis about the chemical transmission of nerve impulses. Elias Howe, who invented the sewing machine, dreamt about how the needle should be formed and how the hole needed to be located at the tip of the needle. And then there is the most famous dream of all: Jacob's Ladder from the book of Genesis. "And in his dream angels of God were ascending and descending on it!" Some interpret the angels in the dream as souls ascending to, and descending from, human bodies on Earth. The place at which Jacob spent the night was Mount Moriah, the future location of the Temple in Jerusalem. The ladder, therefore, symbolizes the "gateway" between Heaven and Earth.

"Humans should not try to interpret their dreams," Elijah went on, raising his voice. "Neither should they try to figure out why a person or a subject came to them in a dream. Rather, they should cooperate and act upon a dream." Then he added in a lower voice, his gaze piercing me, "Human kind will soon progress, advance to a higher level. Humans will then intertwine soul and mind, spirit, and matter, and you will truly become Creator-like."

We sat without speaking for some time.

"You came here to ask me about your son," Elijah said eventually, breaking the silence. "Now I can tell you"—his hand tightened over mine, and it was at that point that I realized he had been holding my hand the entire time—"your son is your father."

I looked at him and then at my dad. I was stunned. I felt elated, and a strange sensation of joy and relief ran through my body; a feeling of revelation washed my whole being. I could not put this feeling into words, but it felt amazing, as if some missing links in my life had been found and put back in place.

Elijah stood up and started walking back into the garden. I got up too, then hesitated and looked at my dad. He was still sitting on the bench. His face emanated calmness and the faint creases of a gentle smile graced his closed eyes. It was time for me to end our journey. It was time for me to return to the lodge.

~~~ — ~~~

"Every soul on Earth, while in a human body, has a purpose—sometimes more than one," he continued. "Once these objectives have been accomplished, the soul then leaves the human body on Earth. In your world, this departure is referred to as dying. In order for a soul to develop, the Creator has given it instruments to work with—the mind and the body, and a path on which to travel—the stages of a life cycle.

~~~ — ~~~

"All human life cycles are similar. The soul and what it needs to accomplish are what makes the difference. For the soul to succeed, it has to maintain a connection with the angels and the Creator. This is what ties the soul to all the resources it needs—energy, healing, love—while it continues its presence on Earth in the human body."

~~~ — ~~~

Chapter Four:

Mind, Body, and Soul

Understanding the wonders of creation, human existence, and the ability to function has preoccupied many people for generations, and I was no exception. I have attended countless discussions and read hundreds of books and articles on these subjects, and yet questions about that mysterious triangle of Mind–Body–Soul and their interdependence remained unanswered.

"What Happened to Sharon?"

Long ago, on a cool summer night on the island of Cyprus, I journeyed for a friend named Tali by the light of the full moon shimmering silver-blue on the waves of the Mediterranean Sea. We were sitting on the sofa in my living room talking about shamanistic practices when suddenly Tali said, "Would you please journey for me to your guides and ask them what happened to Sharon?" She waited silently for my reaction.

I looked at Tali and saw immense grief behind her eyes. I didn't know who Sharon was, but I said, "Sure, let's do it right now."

I closed my eyes, took a deep breath, and began my journey to the Lower World to find Hilla. We met at the same ocean shore with Dolphin and Bear, who had brought me over from the cave. I sat next to Hilla and we watched Dolphin gliding nearby through the waves. Before I had even formulated my question, Hilla said, "He's dead."

I thought I had got used to Hilla's tendency to say unexpected things. But she was still able to surprise me. Taken aback, I looked at her. "He? I thought Sharon was a female," I said. "Dead? Why? How?"

She didn't answer my questions. Instead, I was shown a series of three scenes.

The first scene was at a beach. The sun was going down and a couple was walking along the warm sand holding hands. No one else was there except that couple. I recognized the beach—it was one of Tel Aviv's most beautiful beaches, the same place I used to go swimming every morning on my way to the office just as the sun was rising. The couple appeared to be in their late twenties. She had luminescent white skin; her long blonde hair fell loosely over her shoulders, cascading down her back. He was tall and slim and had dark olive-colored skin. They walked hand in hand, watching as the end of the day transformed into a magical Mediterranean sunset.

The second scene showed the horizon over the Mediterranean as the sun gradually turned crimson and slipped into the sea. The couple walked into a nearby restaurant for dinner. I couldn't see the name of the restaurant. On one wall was a painting in a dark wooden frame of a boat struggling through huge ocean waves. I saw the couple sit side by side in silence; she toyed with her fork, scraping it backwards and forwards across her plate. He was looking down, his right hand resting beside his untouched food. A gloomy

Chapter Four

silence hung in the air, an unvoiced acknowledgement that there wasn't much left to say anymore.

In the third and final scene the couple were back on the beach. By this time, the sun had been totally swallowed by the Mediterranean. He appeared alone, walking along the shore; then he stepped into the sea. She was standing at a distance watching him, waiting for him to turn around and look at her. But he doesn't turn. He continued walking into the sea, and when the water reached his waist, he looked over his shoulder, turning ever so slightly so she could see his face. He raised his right arm slowly out of the water and waved in the air; it was a farewell wave to her. And right before her astonished eyes, he walked further and further into the waiting sea until it completely enveloped him and he disappeared.

I was completely overwhelmed by these scenes. I didn't want to know what Hilla was about to reveal. I was terribly agitated, but I still held on to the visions when I stopped the journey and returned to the room. I opened my eyes and looked at Tali.

"Sharon is a male, right?" I asked after a moment's hesitation.

"Yes," she replied, looking concerned.

"Sharon has gone. He is dead," I said.

"Yes," she replied and tears started to roll down her cheeks.

"He drowned in the sea," I continued.

"Yes," she said through her tears. I held her hands, looked into her eyes, and waited for a while before I shared with her the visions I had just seen.

"That's exactly what happened," Tali said. "But no one knows why. Would you please ask your guides?"

I hesitated at first, not wanting the burden of having to communicate something awful to my friend. But then I took a deep breath and agreed to do it. I closed my eyes and found myself slipping quickly back to where Hilla, Dolphin and Bear were waiting for me. Hilla sat on the sand with Bear lying next to her; Dolphin, a few feet away, slipped silently in and out of the ocean waves.

"Hilla, why did Sharon go?" I asked.

Hilla turned her face towards me, her long, silky, straight, coal-black hair swinging down over her shoulders, and looked at me with a serious expression in her eyes. "His soul couldn't cope anymore. Some souls find this world a searing experience and break down when opposing forces seem to be pulling them in different directions. Their inner framework shatters. His soul just couldn't take it anymore so it decided to leave the Earth."

With a puzzled and heavy heart, I thanked Hilla and returned to Tali. I gently relayed Hilla's explanation for Sharon's departure.

Tears coursed down my friend's pale face. Then she sighed, straightened her shoulders, and reached out to clasp my hands. "He suffered a lot," she said in a broken, tear-filled voice. "He led a double life. He was a well-known and successful film director, but he was also a very religious person, a seeker, and his boundless curiosity drew him to the spiritual world. Those two worlds—film director and spiritual seeker—were extremely different and he was torn by the two different lifestyles. The more successful he became as a film director the closer he drew to spirituality, yet they were incompatible lifestyles. 'Tali, I just can't take it anymore,' he told me the last time I saw him, and then not long afterwards, his body was found washed up on the shore in Tel Aviv. I heard that he had died sometime during the night after he had had dinner with his wife." Tali started to sob again. "Do you think Sharon committed suicide because he couldn't deal with the conflict between the two ways of life anymore?" she asked.

"It certainly wasn't an accident," I replied. "As Hilla said, his soul just couldn't take it anymore so it decided to leave the Earth."

Controller, Carrier, and Passenger

I once read a story in which a young father speaks about his child who died at the age of three months. This young father was familiar with the concept of channeling, and he channeled the spirit world hoping to find comfort, to fill the hole of agony that pierced his being. He later discovered that his child died so young because its soul had accomplished its task and left the Earth. This young father's story made me wonder how significant the role of the soul is in our lives. What is the relationship between the soul and the mind, and how does the body relate to them?

I knew then that I was on a quest, with questions to meditate upon; I was not at the point where I wanted definite answers about the relationship between body, mind, and soul, or about life and death. I just knew that a sense of humble questing drove me to continue my journey.

Bear was in his regular spot next to the cave, sitting on a bed of lush green grass in the magical forest and bathing in the sunlight. I felt tremendous joy to see Bear again. We hugged, I jumped on his back, and he flew me to the beach, where he gently lowered me onto the sand at Hilla's feet. Dolphin was lying at the water's edge, the ocean gently lapping his body, and he looked at us with his beautiful, kind eyes. Hilla, Bear, and Dolphin seemed unusually excited this time. As always, Hilla intuited my questions and my quest.

"Let us journey to the Upper World," she suggested in a soft, loving voice. "We will seek time with Elijah."

I climbed on Bear's glistening snow-white furry back, Dolphin stood upright on his tail, elegantly stretching his sleek gray body above the water, hovering on its surface, and Hilla stood up, raised her hands to the sky, and looked up. That was our sign to ascend to the Upper World, and after we passed through the familiar white membrane of cloud, we landed on the soft cotton-like surface of the White World.

The profound whiteness embraced us as we walked towards the white palace, Hilla on one side of me, Bear on the other, and Dolphin swimming ahead of us. We passed through the palace's open gate and within minutes reached the large white marble table with benches on each side where I usually met Elijah. We sat down and waited, Hilla sitting to my right with her eyes shut. I looked at the palace in the distance; it wasn't revealing much of its glory that day.

I had felt Elijah's presence, but he was nowhere to be seen. All of a sudden, I heard a familiar deep voice: "The mind is the controller, the body is the carrier, and the soul is the passenger. Throughout a life journey, the mind and soul are in constant communication. The life cycle is structured so that the soul is given the opportunity to influence the direction of the life journey at the beginning and at the end, more than at any other stage of the human life cycle. For the soul to learn, develop, and make progress, it needs a mind and a body," Elijah continued. "When the soul decides to go down to Earth, it picks the body and mind that fits its purpose and that best help it to accomplish its tasks for that life journey. So while the soul makes the decision about what type of body and mind it will evolve into, it is mostly the mind that controls the progress itself. It is the mind that mostly influences what the soul will learn."

He paused and remained silent, allowing me to absorb what he had just told me. I was fascinated. I knew from my readings of Hindu sacred literature that it was common practice for the Sadhu (Holy man) to leave his family, his village, and go away on a spiritual journey to seek redemption, and to look for answers to life's purpose and other philosophical questions. I had also heard people saying, when they saw a newborn, "This baby has a pure soul," or "This baby has an old soul." This suggests that people can relate to a baby's soul.

"There are many thoughts about the need to balance body, mind, and soul," I said to Elijah on the other side of the table. His eyes were shut but I knew he was listening, so I continued. "Some say that the balance of body, mind, and soul is the ultimate experience, and that only when all three are balanced can we make the best progress in our lives."

Elijah's head was bowed and a divine, peaceful eminence radiated from him. After a few seconds he replied, "This balance that you humans talk about is different from what the real relationship should be between soul, mind, and body. Since the mind is in control, it may turn out that the soul's ability to function is very limited. This happens mainly when the mind is too much occupied with itself, when one's ego becomes more important than taking care of the body. When that happens, there is often bodily sickness and, later on, a dysfunctional soul, which leads, in some cases, to death, either by suicide or as a result of severe illness."

"So balance is required, but controlled by the mind, which changes as a person's life progresses," I suggested.

"Precisely," he said. "The soul will leave the body—leave Earth—if it feels that the mind is not supporting it anymore, when the mind is not helping it to achieve its goals."

Chapter Four

He paused, opened his eyes and looked straight into mine. His sharp gaze hypnotized me. I could neither think nor move.

"Is that the case when someone has a severe trauma or goes into a coma?" I eventually managed to ask.

Elijah remained silent for a while and then said, "When a human is in a coma, the soul leaves Earth for the Yellow World where it can recover. It may return to the same mind and body in that life cycle or it may decide not to come back at all. When a baby is created, the mind is blank and empty. However, paradoxically, that is also when the mind is best able to absorb knowledge. Then it is the soul's role to record in the mind all it needs to initiate the life journey ahead. All nature's laws, all perceptions, and all reflexes are recorded in the mind when the soul merges with the body. As the child grows, the mind's ability to influence the soul's progress gets stronger. The older the child becomes, the more control the mind has on what the soul is about to experience and learn. The mind is designed in such a way that, from the time the baby is born, certain developments take place through which the soul experiences, learns, and acquires knowledge during its lifetime."

Again, Elijah paused and remained silent for a while. I looked around. Hilla was still at my side, but her eyes were shut while she processed Elijah's teachings.

Then Elijah continued. "As humans get older, the mind becomes more storage-like, in contrast to the emptiness of the receptacle at the baby stage. In later years, information for the soul to process is loaded into the mind to share, from where it will eventually choose what to take as a lesson before it leaves the human body. So while the soul might decide to terminate life at any given stage, it is actually the mind that dictates the life path and, subsequently, the lessons the soul will learn."

A silence ensued as I absorbed these concepts. I looked up at Elijah. His eyes were closed, and though his face reflected a serene calmness, I could feel his powerful presence. He then opened his eyes and looked at me, as if questioning my understanding. I sat motionless, needing to reflect, but I knew the time with Elijah was precious so I asked another question.

"How do the mind and the soul communicate?"

Elijah continued looking at me. I was almost sure I saw a smile in his eyes, something that I rarely saw.

"You're touching on something that very few have knowledge of so far," he eventually said.

I maintained a respectful silence, hoping to hear more.

"The mind has several circuits and uses currents of energy to access them," he went on. "Each one has a certain purpose, and you humans are allowed to access only a few of them—the circuit that controls bodily movements, the circuit that allows you to analyze the circuit of thinking, and some others. While those are significant circuits, there are others that are only used for communication between the soul and the mind. In those particular circuits, the soul stores its experience and knowledge for the mind to act upon. The soul, in order to further develop, will access those circuits when leaving the body and take what it needs. It does this by using the three energy currents—blue, green, and red. The combination of those currents reflects the different types of information the soul processes and communicates with the mind and with the other souls."

I felt as if Hilla was trying to ask something, so I turned to look at her. She opened her eyes, looked at Elijah, and asked, "What is happening to his mind now as he speaks with you?"

This really took me by surprise. Never before had Hilla spoken when we were in the presence of Elijah.

"His mind has shut down, and so has his body," Elijah explained. "And this shutting down causes his soul to function fully and absorb what has been said. Here, in the Upper World, there is no meaning for body and mind, just as there is no meaning for other earthly elements like time and space. Only the soul exists here."

I felt overwhelmed. I had never thought of soul, mind, and body relationships in this way, and I felt that there was so much more Elijah could tell me. I sat motionless, enveloped by a sense of stillness previously unknown to me. I didn't want to leave this magnificent white garden, the white table, and my bench of knowledge. I just wanted to hear more, to absorb, to understand. I didn't want to leave the presence of Elijah.

Then Elijah closed his eyes, bowed his head down to his chest and gradually disappeared into the misty whiteness. In the distance, the palace and its towers slowly became clearer.

"We should return now," I heard Hilla say.

We got up, joined Dolphin and Bear, and returned to the Lower World.

― ― ―

"Throughout a life journey, the mind and soul are in constant communication. The life cycle is structured so that the soul is given the opportunity to influence the direction of the life journey at the beginning and at the end, more than at any other stage of the human life cycle. For the soul to learn, develop, and make progress, it needs a mind and a body,"

― ― ―

"This balance that you humans talk about is different from what the real relationship should be between soul, mind, and body. Since the mind is in control, it may turn out that the soul's ability to function is very limited. This happens mainly when the mind is too much occupied with itself, when one's ego becomes more important than taking care of the body. When that happens, there is often bodily sickness and, later on, a dysfunctional soul, which leads, in some cases, to death, either by suicide or as a result of severe illness."

― ― ―

Chapter Five:

Love and Souls

~~ — ~~

"All you need is love," the immortal song written by John Lennon, contains a simple message for everyone—love is everything; it's all we need.

Is love really all we need? Is it that simple? And what about the concept of a soul mate? Is it also a form of love? All of us at some point in our lives feel a deep connection with someone else that feels different from love, it seems as if we complete each other and share the same path, same destiny; we often call the person we have those feelings for our soul mate. Over a hundred songs were credited to the Lennon–McCartney partnership. Were John and Paul soul mates? Together, they definitely created something magnificent during those years. I was eager to hear from Hilla what she thought about love and soul mates and destiny.

A pine-scented summer breeze wafted through the open door of the living room of my house in the Troodos Mountain. It was a weekend afternoon when I went on my shamanic journey searching for the meaning of love. As I played my drum and shook my rattles, I lay down on the floor and covered myself with a blanket, closed my eyes, and instantly arrived at the hole in the bottom of the ocean to start my water slide ride to the cave. As with all my other journeys, Bear was sitting in his usual spot on a bed of vivid green grass outside the cave in the majestic forest. Effortlessly, I climbed onto his back, slipped my hands deep into his fur and held on tightly while he took me to the beach where Hilla was waiting for me. Dolphin was swimming in the ocean and occasionally hovered on his tail on the surface, waving and smiling at us with his kindly eyes. I sat beside Hilla and soaked up the surrounding energies, enjoying nature's mystical sounds and breathing in the crisp ocean air. Together, Hilla and I sat there facing the clear blue water, Hilla with her eyes shut and me watching Dolphin gambol in the waves.

After a while I turned to look at Hilla, holding my questions in my mind. Before I spoke a word, she said, "You should talk to Elijah about love. Let's go together to meet him."

We stood up and Hilla gestured for me to hold her left hand. Then she raised her right hand up to the sky and looked up. We climbed up instantly, breaking through the white membrane and landing on the soft cotton-like surface of the White World. Profound whiteness embraced us as we walked through the mist towards the palace, Hilla one step behind me to my right.

Elijah was waiting at the palace gate. This was quite unusual, I thought, and again I felt that familiar feeling of immense respect mixed with humility and awe. His magnetic presence overpowered his entire surroundings. His regal appearance always left me amazed and speechless. We arrived at the gate and went into the garden to sit on the bench. Hilla and I faced Elijah and he began his teaching.

Chapter Five

Love

"Love is other than you think it is," said Elijah, looking straight into my eyes. "Love is not what you humans usually refer to as strong feelings towards someone or something. Love is the Creator."

It had been some time now since the first time Elijah and I had met and I didn't feel quite so uncomfortable in his celestial presence. "Love is the Creator?" I repeated, wanting to be sure I had heard him properly.

When I voiced this question, I felt Hilla's warmth flow into me, as if she were trying to help me and give me her support, although no words or looks were exchanged. I was captivated by Elijah's eyes, which were flecked with gray and green and amber. They were magnetic. He smiled at me with his eyes as if reading my soul. I felt as if I was wrapped in a gown of love; I am at a loss to find the words to describe that moment. His silence lapped over me in waves. It felt as if he was waiting for me to fully digest and absorb his answer.

"The Creator, or the divine, is what love is all about," he said, standing up and walking around us, his white gown brushing the ground, his face glowing and his dark eyes piercing me as if he was trying to plant his thoughts in my head.

"The Creator of all this—the universe, the planets, life—is the source of love, the foundation of being, the cause of living. The spirituality of one feeds all physical dimensions. Physical forms cannot exist without spiritual levels. Take the soul away from its body and what do you get?" He calmly sat down again on the bench opposite us. My mind was racing, frantically searching for answers. Then I realized that he probably wasn't really looking for a response. He was planting seeds, seeds of knowledge, and all I had to do was sit and listen.

"Take away the energy of any object and what do you get?" he asked.

I couldn't restrain myself and responded, "So love and energy are the same?"

"Yes, in a way," he replied. "Love, or energy, makes any object alive, makes it function so it will manifest its purpose. Love is the only thing that drives the cyclic motion of the physical and the spiritual worlds. On Earth you are born, you live, die and are born again. Only love can allow that cycle to carry on. Love is the source of it all."

By this time I had got used to hearing unexpected things, so I wasn't at all surprised. But my curiosity created a longing to know more.

If the Creator is love, what is energy? How does it all work, I wondered. I knew something of love, but who was the Creator? How did this all fit into something I already knew about?

"It's simpler than one would think," Elijah said. I was taken aback, for I had only thought my questions, not spoken them. But Elijah smiled, and his eyes radiated bright light, vivid like the stars on a desert night.

"There are other realms where the souls go when they leave the physical body," he continued. "They are transformed, recharged, and immersed in love, almost like an ocean of love, in order to come back and perform the tasks necessary for their development on Earth. Without love, this cycle, this dimension of being, cannot continue. Each realm has different color. The realm we are in is the White World. The realm of love is red."

I kept silent despite having many questions. I could feel my ability to take in what he was saying slowly fade. This was an immense topic. How could I absorb so much?

"You see, you humans refer to love as something that expresses strong feelings towards others, but that is not what love truly is," Elijah said. The significant aspect of love for you is that you feel fulfilled when you love. Experiencing love gives you a glimpse of the Creator and brings you closer to your Creator, closer to the divine."

All you need is love, I thought to myself. Perhaps love *is* actually all that one needs in order to fulfill one's purpose, to create, to become Creator-like.

~~~ — ~~~

"The Creator, or the divine, is what love is all about," he said, standing up and walking around us, his white gown brushing the ground, his face glowing and his dark eyes piercing me as if he was trying to plant his thoughts in my head."

~~~ — ~~~

Chapter Five

Soul Mates

I looked at Hilla and raised my eyebrows, silently seeking her approval to ask Elijah about soul mates and what "soul mate" actually meant. Hilla nodded and as I turned to Elijah, he began to answer my unspoken question.

"Sure, we can talk about soul mates. But first, let me tell you about souls and spirits. Each soul has its purpose in your world. Each soul may return to a human being again and again in order to accomplish its purpose."

"Purpose? How would a soul know its purpose?" I asked.

"While on Earth a soul does not know its purpose, but once it has departed to the other worlds, the soul has clear knowledge of whether it has accomplished its purpose or whether it must come back to Earth."

"So a soul is clueless about its purpose while it's on Earth, but fully aware of it while here in the White World?" I said.

"Correct. Here or in the other worlds, but not while it's on Earth," replied Elijah.

"So what's happening here, or in the other worlds?" I asked.

"Now that you know about the soul's cycle, let's talk about soul mates," Elijah said, ignoring my question. They're not what you think they are. Soul mates are souls that work together to achieve a distinct purpose. Soul mates might partner for a long time—months, perhaps years—or a short time—days, hours, minutes even. The length of time soul mates are together is meaningless. What's more important is the goal they need to achieve."

I was intrigued. What I had just heard didn't fit my idea of what soul mates were.

"In fact, there are examples of short encounters that were more meaningful to the two souls than long encounters were," Elijah continued. "Furthermore, a soul may have many soul mates while on Earth. It is all depends on the stage that the soul is at and the mission it has to accomplish at that stage."

Elijah paused, giving me time for reflection.

On Earth, we humans perceive a soul mate as a love connection, a bond between two people that we often can't explain and that sometimes has little to do with what we humans call love. A person may have a once-in-a-lifetime encounter with another person and it may only be for a short period of time—an hour, a weekend—yet it can completely change those peoples' lives thereafter. We often use the term "soul mate" in the context of "falling in love" or when expressing strong feelings of attraction. But Elijah was suggesting that the concept of soul mates has a different meaning and can manifest in different ways. If a soul seeks growth and development, the soul's encounters do not always have to be harmonious ones.

Elijah looked at me while I thinking, and it seemed that he was reading my thoughts. "Having a soul mate is very significant to any soul," he said. "In many cases, a soul's purpose can't be achieved without connecting with a soul mate to help."

Perhaps that's what people mean when they say that soul mates are like two wings of a bird, I thought—both must be strong for the bird to fly.

"Soul mates are souls that work together to achieve a distinct purpose. Soul mates might partner for a long time—months, perhaps years—or a short time—days, hours, minutes even."

Destiny

I returned to my conversation with Elijah. This time I spoke first.

"I understand that souls have a purpose. I understand that they keep coming back until they fulfill that purpose. But what is a soul's destiny? When a soul fulfills a purpose, what happens then?" I asked.

Elijah sat back for a moment and then leaned forward, squinting at me as if assessing my ability to understand what he was about to reveal.

"There is no such thing as soul's destiny," he said eventually. "I'll explain to you later what happens to a soul once it achieves its purpose."

He paused again. I looked at him without saying a word, and waited patiently for him to continue.

"A human being's destiny is the outcome of the soul's purpose. While a soul's purpose is clearly known, a human being's destiny is unknown, for it is determined by the path that the soul takes and that path could be influenced by other souls, such as soul mates. A human being's destiny is also determined by the mind, which influences the soul and which depends on the life stage—infant, child, adult, elderly—the human is at."

Plain Souls

"There are three different levels of souls," Elijah explained. "Plain souls are the first level. They still haven't accomplished their purpose; plain souls have to come back to Earth again and again until all lessons have been learned and all purposes achieved. Every stage in the growth of the physical body teaches them something new, and they may make progress every time they come back to Earth. When they leave Earth, they go up to the Red World to be healed, to recover, to get help, to learn, and to rest. When they are ready, those souls will come back to Earth, back to a physical human body."

"Could you share an example of a soul that has not accomplished its purpose on Earth?" I asked tentatively, worried that I was being too forthright.

"Suicide," replied Elijah. "When a soul is under tremendous stress, feels trapped, and is unable to cope with a certain situation, it gives up. That soul will then instruct the human's mind to kill the body so it can leave. This soul will be led to the Red World to recover from the trauma, and will then be assisted by the angels to study and learn from its experiences. It will see the pattern of its life more clearly, and come to understand what went wrong and how to deal with the situation in a better way. Once the soul is ready it will leave the Red World and return in a physical human form to the earthly sphere, where it will experience a similar situation to which it had previously responded poorly. In this way, a soul gains strength to enable it to move to the next stage of growth."

Angels

"Angels are the second level of souls. They are souls who have accomplished their purpose and may decide not to return to Earth, but to stay in the Red World. Souls which have reached this level are ready to help the plain souls, either on Earth or while they are in the Red World. However, angels may choose to return to Earth in a human body to become a soul mate to plain souls. Angels can also go to Earth as spirits, rather than in a physical form, to help plain souls attain their purpose."

Questions flew out of my mouth. "Do we see these angels? Can we talk to them—pray to them?"

"Yes," replied Elijah to my hurried questions. "When a human calls an angel it is actually the human soul that needs help, support, or advice. This 'calling upon the angel' happens mostly while the human is asleep, in the world of dreams, since only while sleeping is the soul free to connect with angels or other non-human helpers."

"Free of what?" I asked.

"Free of coping with the human mind," replied Elijah.

It's amazing, I thought to myself. I need to journey some more with Elijah on the topic of souls and the mind. I looked him, hoping for a sign of agreement.

"Indeed," he said. "Let's walk on it."

I thought I saw him smiling, but it might have been my imagination.

Prophets

"The third level of souls are the prophets," continued Elijah. "Those souls always stay in the Upper World and never return to Earth. Angels may choose to become prophets or stay angels. Prophets help angels, and may choose to guide and assist the plain souls while they are on Earth in various ways—prayer, meditation, shamanic journey, and other similar methods."

"Like you and me?" I asked.

Rarely did I see any expression on Elijah's face, let alone a smile. This time, however, he opened his eyes, looked straight at me and smiled kindly. "Like me and you—the prophet and the shaman."

I felt as if my entire body has been washed with pure love. It was blissful; I was in heaven.

Chapter Six:

The Ten Soul Commandments

When I was growing up in Kibbutz Givat Brener, the radio was the most popular form of entertainment for a small kid. We had a library in an impressive two-story marble building called Bet-Sirenie that was located on a hill in the center of our kibbutz.

On one side, a small forest of towering eucalyptus trees, one of my favorite hideouts, bounded Bet-Sirenie. On the other side was a large, dark green lawn, the size of two football fields combined, and in the far corner, vibrant water lilies—white, yellow, pink—floated in a small heart-shaped fishpond that was sheltered by tall bamboo trees. Green frogs hopped in and out of the pond, and the most well-fed golden carp I have ever seen swam leisurely in it.

"Hush! Keep Quiet" said the wooden sign that hung on the front door of the library. A long corridor ran from the library's entrance, its walls lined with photos of the kibbutz's founders, and it led to a big hall with a few tables and tall bookshelves with all kinds of books on history and astrology. Once a week, on a Friday night, we had a movie night; most of the movies were R-rated. I would hide outside in the dark and sneak into the theater as soon as the lights went off. Nothing held back my rebellious streak. I loved to challenge adults' rules.

But the ultimate pleasure for me was sitting in front of the radio listening to broadcasts of any kind. It was the highlight at the end of every day. At night, after homework and after my shower, I'd put a headset over my ears to shut out the outside world and dive into a magical ocean of sounds and frequencies.

When I was nine I built my own radio, and oh boy, was I proud! I constructed a small wooden box with two brown wooden dial-type knobs on the front, one for volume and the other for channel selection. To the back of the box I wired an antenna, which I connected with the roof of our house. To the left of the radio, I connected a headset I found at a flea market in Rehovot, a neighboring town.

I remember spending hours listening to various of programs broadcast by different radio stations—the *Hourly News*, and *Dash Im Shir*, a program of blessings and songs, on Galei Tzahal; documentaries, and drama series like *Mishpachat Simchon*, the story of an Israeli family, on Kol Israel; *Popular Songs Hit Parade* on Radio Ramallah.

But there was only one program that made me feel inspired, that touched me deeply and made me think and wonder, that made me feel that I was nurturing my soul. Every Friday after sunset, I'd go to my tiny bedroom, sit on my bed, and reach out my hand to switch off the lamp. I'd shut my eyes and listen to the weekly Torah reading, *Parashat Hashavuah*. I have been always fascinated by the Torah stories, like those found in the book of Genesis, the story of Joseph in Egypt, and myriad others. But most of all I was intrigued and inspired by Moses the Prophet. He was a humble man who had a stammer. He could hardly talk, yet he was chosen by God to

Chapter Six

lead the entire nation of Israelites out of Egypt on what became a forty-year journey to the Promised Land.

Many years later, when I was in my late forties and was living in the small village of Saitas in the Troodos Mountains, I was strolling along a trail in the ancient black pine tree forest on one foggy Saturday at dawn. It was part of my weekend morning ritual. I would wake up at dawn and walk through the forest, taking deep breaths of the crisp morning air, enjoying nature's magnificence and admiring the majesty of the mountains. It's amazing how harmonious nature is, I thought as I watched a rabbit dig a hole in the ground under a small bush, while a couple of mouflon (kind of wild sheep only found in Cyprus) crossed the trail, and a hawk cruised above searching for breakfast. It was serene, almost surrealistic, yet peaceful. I felt as if I had witnessed a divine symphony in a most sacred concert hall.

That morning I had taken the Book of Torah with me. I planned to read at some point on the trail. That particular week, the weekly Torah reading was "Parashat Yithro" (part of Torah named after Yithro, Moses' father-in-law) from the book of Exodus. It begins with the story of Moses' father-in-law, Yithro, who came to visit Moses in the Sinai Desert. Yithro brought Tzipporah, Moses' wife, who had been sent home to her father earlier, along with her two sons, Gershom and Eliezer. It goes on to tell the heroic story of how Moses received the Ten Commandments.

As I reached my favorite spot on the trail, the morning fog had lifted, allowing the sun to warm the mountain air and waken the plants. In the distance I could see sunlight sparkling on the blue waters of the Mediterranean, framed by the glorious Troodos Mountains that were covered with the lavish green tapestry of black pine trees. I took a deep breath of the fresh mountain air and lowered myself onto a grassy spot by the tree. To my right, down below, I could see the village of Omodos, famous for its wine production, with its painted blue and white houses and narrow paved streets. I felt my bones settling into the earth as I opened the Torah and started reading "Parashat Yithro." I reached verse 20 where God comes down to Earth: "God came down on Mount Sinai, to the peak of the mountain."

As I read, something strange happened. I felt Elijah calling me, though the only sound I could actually hear was the sound of the wind blowing through trees. But the strong feeling didn't subside or go away. I stopped reading and closed my eyes. Elijah's face vividly appeared. I felt his strong gaze upon my face, but he kept silent. He looked at me as if waiting for me to say or to do something. I leaned back, lay down on the ground, and placed the Torah on my chest. Suddenly, in an instant, I found myself standing next to Elijah near the majestic white garden in front of the white palace.

Elijah looked sort of grandfatherly with snowy white hair and a white beard. His eyes, two dark shining diamonds, radiated eminent wisdom and divinity, like wells of knowingness. He walked towards the marble bench, sat on it, and turned to look up at me standing on the other side of the white marble table. He smiled; deep lines creased around his mouth. He then beckoned me to sit on the bench opposite him, and reached out his right hand towards me. I felt his grasp; my hand lay in his hand and it felt safe. He rested his hands on the top of the marble table while I put my hands, still warm from Elijah's touch, on the table. He greeted me. I knew he was going to speak about the Ten Commandments; why, I don't know, but I knew this.

"The Creator decided to establish order in the chaos," Elijah said. "The Israelites were to be given a set of fundamental rules for how they should treat themselves and each other, and how they should treat nature." Elijah paused and looked at me closely. What he saw must have pleased him because he continued. "The Creator wanted to make the Israelites realize the significance of this phase in human society's evolution—the transformation, via a new set of rules, from a state of instinct and nature to a civilization guided by intellectual and moral values. So he came down to Mount Sinai, covering the mountain top with a cloud, to deliver those rules to Moses. Through fire and smoke, he directed Moses to share this knowledge with his people so they would then pass on those rules and values to other nations."

I sat there in front of that holy man and my mind was blank. I couldn't take my eyes off his face, which glowed against the white surroundings. It's difficult to describe other-worldly things in words, but at that moment I felt as if we were in the most purified white

Chapter Six

atmosphere, and that the white was celestial, without comparison or counterpart on Earth. I couldn't think at all. I just gazed upon his face. Then he smiled, placed his two hands on the big white marble table, got up, and signaled me to follow him. I got up slowly; I was shaking. Questions raced through my mind—where are we going? What for?

Elijah walked towards the magnificent white palace with its seven towers along the front. I could see their tops, but I couldn't see any doors or windows. I followed. As we crossed the beautiful garden, an unearthly tall white orchid bowed to Elijah, and white tulip-shaped plants showered snowflakes on the trail before him as if blessing his path. Hypnotized by this majestic vision, I followed a few steps behind Elijah to the central tower, which was tall and round and, like all the other towers, had no doors or windows. Elijah continued walking straight into and through the thick marble wall of the tower.

I hesitated and looked around, wondering what to do. Should I follow him through that thick wall? I could see him walking on the other side of it. He didn't stop and he didn't turn around. So I followed through, exactly as he had done, perhaps feeling a little fearful. I continued following in Elijah footsteps. As I passed through, I paused to look behind me. I could see the garden and the white table. It was amazing—to be surrounded by see-through, walk-through walls!

I picked up my pace—I didn't want to lose Elijah. He continued steadily on in the distance and then went down a long corridor. I followed him a bit more quickly. To our right was the tower wall and to our left was a small empty courtyard with a floor that seemed to be made of white cotton. On the other side of the courtyard, huge white silky curtains moved gently; they were so large, I couldn't see the top of them. The silky curtains rippled like a waterfall flowing from an unseen top down into the white cotton-like floor. It was a magnificent scene. I wanted to stay and absorb this scene, but I had to hurry to catch up with Elijah. He was constantly moving and after what seemed like a long time he stopped. His white hair and beard swayed gently as he turned to look back, waiting for me.

As soon as I reached his side, he grabbed my arm. I felt a warm electric current rushing through me. I looked at him but he remained silent. He was looking ahead. Was he waiting for someone or something? A few minutes passed, Elijah still firmly holding my arm. Then I saw a beam of light. I couldn't see its source, but its light fell on the ground just a few steps in front of us. Was this what Elijah had been waiting for? I was conscious of his firm but gentle grip on my arm, and together we went towards this beam of light. When we reached the spot on the ground where the light fell, Elijah paused. It took me few seconds to realize that we were no longer on the ground. The light beam carried us up and away from the palace corridor. I was shocked and excited at the same time.

A few seconds later the light beam placed us on a round, white, smooth, bare surface. I saw no sign of the palace, only cotton-like clouds beneath us; the light beam remained under our feet. I looked up, trying to follow the beam of light to its source, but all I could see were the cotton-like clouds and the light stretching into endless white. I could still feel Elijah's protective grip and I looked at him. He stood erect with his eyes shut. His white cotton gown covered him from his shoulders to his feet, and his long white hair and beard almost covered his face. He radiated greatness, glory, and grace.

> *"The Creator wanted to make the Israelites realize the significance of this phase in human society's evolution—the transformation, via a new set of rules, from a state of instinct and nature to a civilization guided by intellectual and moral values."*

First and Second Soul Commandments

"I am God your Lord, who brought you..."
"Do not have any other gods before me."

Elijah raised his right hand and, pointing at the ray of light, said, "Man was created by the Creator's form." He paused for a second before continuing. "In the first two commandments, the Creator revealed himself to Moses as his Creator, his only source of empowerment, comprehension, and spirituality." Again Elijah paused, then went on. "The first two commandments instruct Man to route his mind and awareness inward, into his life force, to the Creator, in order to make mankind aware of its soul, which is the channel through which Man connects to the Creator."

Elijah turned towards me and opened his eyes, revealing his boundless wisdom; his eyes pierced my soul. Shivering, I stood next to him trying to comprehend what I had just heard. Somehow I found the courage to ask, "Was that the first time the Creator made Man aware of his soul?"

"Correct," replied Elijah. "The Creator wanted to bring the soul's existence into Man's awareness, to bring it to his attention."

Third Soul Commandment

"Do not take the name of God, your Lord, in vain."

Then Elijah turned back to the beam of light, raised his hand again, and said: "In the third commandment, the Creator told Moses that Man's soul is pure and means no harm." Elijah paused; he was still pointing at the light with one hand and holding me firmly by the arm with his other hand. "No soul is evil; no soul is immoral. A man should not search elsewhere for truth other than inside himself, because the Creator is in Man's own soul." Elijah paused again, laid his right hand on his chest, his palm over his heart, then bowed his head and shut his eyes.

I froze. My head was heavy and my legs weak. If it hadn't been for Elijah's reassuring grip on my arm, I would have been unable to stand. I could neither think nor speak.

Fourth Soul Commandment

"Remember the Sabbath…"

"The fourth commandment was intended to give mankind a break from daily routines and the opportunity to connect with and nurture his soul," Elijah continued, keeping his right hand raised towards that light. "By creating time free of day-to-day distractions, Man can grow spiritually and develop his soul. Whether that time is short or long, it allows Man to connect with the Creator through his soul, thus giving the soul the space to remember its purpose, the reason it came to Earth."

Elijah stopped. His voice was becoming weaker, and his grasp on my arm was not so firm. What had he been through? I wondered. Why had we come here to stand in this place surrounded by white clouds and with that beam of light? Where does the light come from and why? Those questions pounded in my head as we stood in the vast silence.

Elijah didn't say a word, but he remained standing by my side, his face and hand pointing towards the light.

Fifth, Sixth, Seventh, Eighth, Ninth, and Tenth Soul Commandments

"Honor your father and your mother…"
"Do not commit murder."
"Do not commit adultery."
"Do not steal."
"Do not testify false…"
"Do not be envious…"

"The first four commandments relate to Man's relations with his soul and with the Creator," Elijah said unexpectedly. "The other six commandments relate to the soul's interaction with other souls, and are intended to give Man knowledge of other souls' needs in order teach him to be aware of those around him. Family members, friends, neighbors—all are alike; they are all souls sharing the same basic needs, and they are all on Earth to develop and progress by implementing these fundamental moral rules given to Moses by the Creator. The last six commandments instruct Man not to obstruct or deter other souls from accomplishing their purpose."

Chapter Six

I looked at Elijah. He lowered his right hand to his side and bowed his head. I knew it was over, and I felt calm and peaceful.

I was just beginning to process what I had heard, when the beam of light slowly lifted us and carried us back to the white palace's long, white corridor, where Elijah eventually let go of my arm. We passed by the courtyard, went back through the wall of the tower, walked through the garden, and took our places on each side of the white table.

I waited for Elijah to speak. He sat with his hands on the white marble top, one hand on top of the other, and his eyes shut. Eventually he said, "Submitting to the Ten Commandments is one of the most significant things humanity can do in order to be better human beings." Then he got up, turned towards the palace, and walked away.

I felt no fear; I just wanted to stay there in that magical place, to hear more, to learn more. Then I opened my eyes to find myself back on my blanket in the Troodos Mountains under the shade of the pine tree. I looked up at the clear blue sky above me; sunlight fell on the hill in front of me; in the distance I could see Omodos's central square humming with visitors.

I sat up, leaning against the tree trunk, and continued to read "Parashat Yithro" from the line my finger was lying on, verse 17: "Do not be afraid," said Moses to the people. "God only came to raise you up. His fear will then be on your faces, and you will not sin."

I closed the book and I thought about what my Spiritual Teacher, Elijah the Prophet, had just taught me. It fitted that verse so well; it made perfect sense.

If only all men and women could be aware of their souls, could connect with them and follow the ten rules the Creator had given to Moses—"God only came to raise you up. His fear will then be on your faces…"—then all human kind would avoid doing wrong—"and you will not sin."

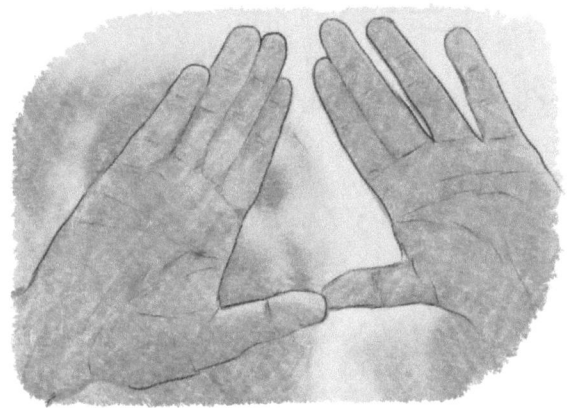

Chapter Seven:

Role of the Complementing Opposites

~~~ — ~~~

Like others, I've had my share of happiness and sadness. The coexistence of positive and negative, along with good and bad, preoccupies many people. For generations, people have watched the seesaw dance of light and darkness, like ocean waves ebbing and flowing on the shore. How is it we live in a world of opposites? What is the purpose of this? Why do we experience ups and downs? What is the role of evil? These were questions that perplexed me.

~~~ — ~~~

"The New World": Symphony No. 9 (Dvořák)

I was driving through the freezing rain of a dark, ice-covered street of midtown St. Louis. Why had I been so willing to give up sitting in my cozy apartment to risk driving on a bad stormy night? I just couldn't miss the opportunity to attend a concert of the St. Louis Symphony Orchestra, that's why! As I drove down Lindell Boulevard towards Grand Avenue and headed towards Powell Hall, home to the STL Symphony, I was full of joy and excitement, for on that evening's program was Antonín Dvořák's wonderful "New World Symphony"—Symphony No. 9.

Next to Antonio Vivaldi, Dvořák is one of my favorite composers. According to classical music historians, Dvořák was fascinated and inspired both by Native American music and the resonating soul of African-American folk culture. When Dvořák wrote Symphony No. 9 he embodied the essentials of these two cultures. He used their themes as subjects, all the while transforming their characteristic sounds into modern rhythms and glorious classical symphonies.

A passion for classical music had developed in me as I grew older, but it had been planted in my soul a long ago, during my childhood when I lived on the kibbutz. Every weeknight around 9 p.m., Shaul, my charismatic Italian step-dad, would brew a strong aromatic espresso and pour it into two small white porcelain cups, one for him and one for me. He would skim the cream from the top of a glass jar full of fresh milk and stir it gently into each espresso cup. My step-dad was very proud of his coffee. I know now that it's not very appropriate for ten-year-olds to drink espresso, especially at night time, but I just loved this ritual. Besides, he always added extra cream to my cup.

"Doobusie," he would call me. "Andiamo, it's opera time." He would then sit next to the radio on his favorite old brown leather striped couch, wrapped in his green flannel robe. I would sat on the carpet at his feet, my espresso cup in my hands, and together we immersed ourselves in an enchanted hour of opera. My step-dad was a hard worker; he was the kibbutz handyman, fixing broken furniture and loose doors and windows, building toys for kids whose parents couldn't afford to buy new ones. He helped everyone beyond the call of duty. We weren't very well off, but my step-dad cherished those few moments of pleasure every evening, and it was a habit I picked up from him, as well as his passion for strong espresso!

Chapter Seven

He treasured all kind of classical music, but most of all he loved the opera. His favorite was Puccini's *Madame Butterfly*. I can still vividly picture him lying on that old brown couch, his arms passionately conducting the unseen orchestra, his eyes closed, his body giving in to the warm embrace of that old leather and a delighted smile spreading across his face as soon as the nightly opera broadcast began. The vibrant voices mixed in perfect harmony with the nighttime sounds of nature that filled our living room.

In addition to the weeknight opera, I loved to listen to the radio on Saturday mornings for a couple of hours when *The Weekly Musical Riddle* was broadcast by Kol Israel. Each week, listeners were challenged with a musical riddle—a short extract from a classical piece. They then had to name the composer and the piece and call the radio station with the answers. Every Saturday, four members from our kibbutz orchestra, Kibbutz Givat Brener Quartet, got together to try to solve the riddle. Of course, my step-dad and I would try to solve this riddle too—well, it was mainly him—and we weren't always successful. But our house rang out with pride and joy every time our kibbutz's team answered correctly—and they won quite often.

On those weekend mornings I was introduced to wonderful masterpieces like Vivaldi's Four Seasons, Mahler's Symphony No. 9, Dvořák's Symphony No. 9 ("New World"), Beethoven's Symphony No. 3 ("Eroica"), and countless others. And so it happened that during those serene musical hours, seeds were planted in my soul, seeds of passion and devotion to classical music. So freezing weather was not going to keep me away from this Dvořák masterpiece.

Evidently, I wasn't the only one undeterred by sheets of icy rain. Powell Hall's lobby resembled the Palace of Versailles—gorgeous rows of crystal chandeliers with tiers of candles hung from an ornate plaster ceiling, under which an expectant audience, wall-to-wall classical music devotees, waited. The warm auditorium seemed like a fairytale world of French wealth; above the audience, a great dome with ornate patterns painted in gold leaf dominated the ceiling; the balcony rails had small curtains that were topped with red velvet.

I relaxed in my seat and waited, full of anticipation for the upcoming concert. The first violinist, the cellist, and the horn section all quietly stepped on stage and took their seats to begin tuning their instruments. Minutes later, Powell Hall's lights slowly dimmed; people's backs straightened in their seats, there were a few last-minute coughs, and a rustle as cell phones were turned off. The concert was about to begin.

The quiet that descends just before a concert begins is almost sacred; it's a portentous silence, presaging something great. Rapturous applause broke out that night as the maestro stepped in front of the orchestra, faced the audience, and bowed, then turned to the orchestra. He raised his baton, nodded to the first violinist, and the harmonious sound of the strings playing the symphony's first movement filled the concert hall.

Adagio

I felt relaxed, took a deep quiet breath, and closed my eyes as I always do when I want to fully experience the music without any visual distractions. Within seconds, I dove into a deep ocean of vibration and sound, and felt as if I was inside the sounds—round and tubular, with the lacework of the strings—that took me on a winding, haunting journey. The waves of sound filled my entire being and lifted me up where I fused with the high sounds of the flute, whose notes touched the ornate ceiling and quietly settled down into the rapt audience. The oboes' low tones vibrated through the floor and I could almost feel the wood of the instruments sending those sounds into my heart.

Suddenly, Powell Hall dissolved in a mist and I found myself in the familiar haze of the White World standing in front of the giant marble white gate. I was mesmerized and it was with great anticipation that I stepped through the open gate into the garden and sat on the white bench to wait for Elijah to show up. While I waited I looked around me. The most amazing landscaping I'd ever seen surrounded me. The lush white blossoms of giant orchids graced the area next to the gate; to my far right, facing the palace, I saw roses with heart-shaped petals; next to the white marble table I noticed small white tulip-shaped plants, their petals sprinkled with snowflakes that seemed to flow out from their centers. The garden seemed real, alive, filled with kinetic energy, and yet it was extremely peaceful and calm. There was no sky and no sun, and there wasn't a sound. All I could hear was the last chords of Dvořák's "Adagio."

Largo

I was flushed with an immense sense of happiness, while calmness washed over me as if I had been showered by crystalline light. I felt my entire body light up. Then I saw him.

Elijah came towards me from a great distance, and then he was quickly by my side. I had a sense that he was floating on the invisible sound wave of the symphony's clarinets. My eyes closed in reverence, and an intention formed deep within me to let all my senses connect to his divine vision and sound. As if Elijah had read my mind and knew about my unanswered questions, he began speaking in a measured tone.

"All opposites—light and darkness, good and bad—exist on Earth for one main reason. This principle is fundamental in nature." Elijah sounded as if he was sitting at the other side of the table. I opened my eyes to see him resting his hands on the big white table. He had his eyes closed and I quickly closed mine again.

"Yes, I know what you people think," he continued. "You learn to appreciate the good by experiencing the bad, but in fact it hasn't much to do with humans. It has a whole lot to do with nature itself."

I kept my eyes shut, realizing that my ability to listen and concentrate was intensified.

"For nature to sustain, evolve, and stay alive, it needs opposites that complement each other, a cyclic movement, a rotation of those opposites," Elijah went on. "Nature needs light and it needs its complement, darkness. To progress, nature also needs love and kindness, and their opposites, hate and cruelty. Creation and destruction are essential for nature as a whole, but specifically to provide a way for humans to progress. Creation and destruction are the basic elements upon which nature is built, and all the other opposites—light, darkness, wet, dry, good, bad—are just part of the spectrum of the creation–destruction cycle."

He paused, allowing me to digest what I just heard before he continued. A human being is part of nature, I thought. Humans can transcend nature because they have a rational mind. We humans have bad days and good days. We all have good things in us, but we also have dark sides. They are parts of the whole, parts of who we are.

"Those opposites are indeed essential and complement each other," Elijah said, reading my mind as usual. "For nature to exist and evolve, it must encompass both polarities, creation and destruction, and in order to nourish itself, each individual living thing must also encompass the two essential elements. Fire may burn and keep you warm on cold nights, but fire can also burn out of control and cause death and destruction. It's the same with water, an essential element for all living forms, but water can also be devastating."

"All opposites—light and darkness, good and bad—exist on Earth for one main reason. This principle is fundamental in nature." Elijah sounded as if he was sitting at the other side of the table. I opened my eyes to see him resting his hands on the big white table. He had his eyes closed and I quickly closed mine again.

Scherzo

It can't be that simple, I thought, and opened my eyes. Nature had always seemed more complicated to me. I looked at Elijah. His eyes were shut and his face radiated immense glory; his hands lay peacefully on the flat white marble table top in front of him. In his presence the background always disappeared; he fills up the whole scene.

"Right, it isn't that simple," I heard Elijah say. "Complementing each other doesn't mean that they exist separately from each other. On the contrary, within every evil there is some kindness; in every light there is darkness; in any act of madness there is some measure of sense. Nothing is just pure light or darkness; nothing is all good or all bad. When you hear laughter, you may also detect the sound of grief."

He stopped speaking. All I could hear was the sound of the orchestra's strings and the flutes echoed by a triangle. I looked at Elijah's face and was overcome by his majestic divinity. Then he opened his eyes, two dark shining diamonds radiating with wisdom, and looked straight into mine. My chest constricted; I could hardly breathe. And then I felt a huge stream of energy flow from those remarkable eyes, washing my inner and outer body with celestial kindness. I still couldn't breathe or move. I felt as if I was held captive by some incredible power, all the while feeling its heavenly blessing.

Allegro

"Hold your hands in front of you," Elijah commanded, "palms facing me, your thumbs pointing inward towards each other and both index fingers reaching upwards, towards each other but not touching. Form an open-top triangle with your two thumbs and index fingers."

I obeyed. Silently I stretched my hands in front of me at shoulder level and with my palms facing Elijah, I formed an open-top triangle. Through the triangle I could see Elijah's shining eyes.

Back in the concert hall the sound of the trumpet vanquished the symphony's strings just at that moment.

Elijah closed his eyes. "Now, that is what nature is all about," he said. "Your hands are making the shape of an open-top triangle, a symbol of nature's three main elements. One side, the triangle's base at the bottom, is the source from where all living things originate, and each side of the triangle represent the other two elements, the positive and the negative—the opposites. The triangle's base, where your thumbs form a solid line, provides a strong support to all of nature's other components. It is the foundation that initiates all nature's elements, and continues to share them as they evolve. And as nature's elements evolve, while they might be different, they remain connected through the base, since they all share the same basic needs. They will not be able to keep on evolving unless they follow nature's directives, which are written in the source. On each side of the triangle, marked by your index fingers, are the opposites, the complement entities in nature. One side is the positive and the other side is the negative. They both share the source, where all are the same and where everything originates, but as nature evolves, these complementing entities form an almost perfect triangle. The distance between positive and negative becomes smaller, as if they eager to unite, but they never will. They remain uniquely defined entities, positive and negative."

Fascinated, I looked at my hands, but before I could say anything, Elijah continued, "Your hands form a shape representing what nature is. It is within this perfect form that living things exist and where basic needs are shared, yet at the same time they are different and complement one another. They are each well defined and yet dependent on the other. Therefore, these living elements can continue to perfect themselves, and just as your two index fingers are almost touching to make a perfect triangle, so living forms will continue to evolve forever, while positive and negative will remain uniquely defined entities."

Elijah paused as if waiting for my response. I rested my hands on the big white table and closed my eyes to help me assimilate his teaching. It's so ironic, I thought to myself, that we strive to be happy, yet sadness is just as important to our self-development, and that we struggle to satisfy our desires, yet failing to achieve them plays a significant role in our growth. I opened my eyes. Elijah had disappeared and I found myself alone in that heavenly garden. I knew I must return to Powell Hall.

I slowly returned to the concert hall as the last sounds of the "Allegro," the final movement of the "New World" symphony, were being played, and just as the thunderous applause began.

I opened my eyes and joined the audience in a standing ovation. My whole body was shaking as my mind continued to process the journey I had just experienced. I looked up and for a few seconds I saw a huge funnel, its top surrounded by white cloud and its bottom hanging right above my seat. But it evaporated into the glittery warm light of Powell Hall's crystal chandeliers.

What was the importance of Dvořák's Symphony No. 9 in teaching me about the role of complementary opposites? Would I ever find out? I certainly felt there was a purpose to it and to my attending this particular concert on that particular night. Regardless of the connection with Dvořák, I now understood that good and bad have equally significant roles to play in nature and in human development.

We all rely on and share the same basic foundation—we live by a set of common rules—but in order to accomplish our individual soul's purpose, each one of us needs to walk through both light and darkness. We need to experience both the good and the bad, and only then, through that cyclic movement, through the rotation of opposites, will we continue to evolve.

"Your hands form a shape representing what nature is. It is within this perfect form that living things exist and where basic needs are shared, yet at the same time they are different and complement one another. They are each well defined and yet dependent on the other."

Chapter Eight:

Divining the Truth

Since the dawn of humanity, mystical, divine, and supernatural phenomena have fascinated us. Unable to rationalize or explain them, some say, "God acts in mysterious ways," others claim, "It is all from God."

Sufism, Kabbalah, and mysticism within religion have always fascinated me. During my childhood in the kibbutz, being close to nature was my favorite way of spending time, either taking care of my bees and my pigeons, playing with my dogs and my rabbits, wandering in the eucalyptus forest, or walking through the orange groves. Living in the countryside stimulated feelings in me that I have not experienced anywhere else. I felt inner joy, a closeness and connection to something pure and extremely powerful, but it was something that as a child I could not comprehend.

As I got older, I searched, read, and discussed a myriad of ideas and perceptions with the like-minded people that I met at shamanism workshops and in India. The more I delved into the mystic realm of ancient philosophies, the more I realized how little I knew and how much more there was to be explored.

Divination

On a warm spring Friday morning, I started my long ride from St. Louis, Missouri, to Washington D.C., anxious to attend an Advanced Shamanic Divination workshop. About a month earlier my good friend Dana had sent me an invitation. The topic of shamanic divination excited me, and I had immediately registered for this weekend-long event.

It had been a while since Dying and Beyond, the last shamanic workshop I had attended at the Pine Tree Lodge near Washington D.C. Since then, I had journeyed countless times for members of my family, for friends, for strangers, but I clearly recalled that first mesmerizing journey to my deceased father, which had happened when I had last been at Pine Tree Lodge. The opportunities to develop my shamanic practice and to meet my dear friend Dana once again got me excited. Besides being a wonderful person and a good friend, Dana is a remarkable facilitator, and I was inspired by his commitment and dedication to shamanic practice.

The twelve-hour ride was smooth along the I-70, and incredible feelings of freedom and bliss washed over me as I passed through the states of Illinois, Indiana, and Ohio. By late evening, I pulled into Dana's apartment parking lot. He lived about forty minutes away from the small cabin in the woods where the workshop was to take place, and had insisted that I stay at his place. We could have breakfast and drive together to the workshop in the morning. Light rain washed the willow trees along the street as I parked my car and knocked on Dana's house door.

Dana's presence filled the doorframe, and we hugged.

"C'mon," he said, walking across his living room to his office where wide windows looked out on a sloping green lawn. "This

Chapter Eight

will be your room for the weekend. The couch pulls out," he said, pointing to a black leather couch. "I hope this will work for you."

"Don't worry, my friend," I replied, chuckling. "I served in the army where I slept in some gruesome places. It can't be worse than sleeping on desert dunes."

I looked around the room. An old cashmere rug covered half of the wooden floor and a round glass-topped table was loaded with Smithsonian magazines. Bookshelves packed with shamanic and other anthropology books were mounted on the wall over Dana's desk.

"This office seems like nirvana to me," I said. We both laughed.

"I guess you must be hungry. What would you like to eat? As I recall, you had a love affair with seafood New Orleans-style," he said with a half grin and twinkly eyes.

"You're right!" I replied, laughing, but I was touched that he'd remembered the first time we met in New Orleans.

"Well, I'll never forget your first shamanic workshop. You came for good food and left hooked on shamanism," he said.

"You changed my life, Dana," I said, looking straight at him. "Thanks to you I live a more meaningful life. After I graduated college I joined the corporate world and as my professional career developed I drifted away from nature, my childhood passion. But now I feel it, living and breathing, as if nature is closer to me than my life's blood. There are so many colorful dimensions with such deep meaning in our lives, and I now live a deeper kind of life in many of those dimensions. My world is very different now than it was then."

"It's yourself who you should be thankful to for being open to this journey," Dana said. "You entered this path knowing nothing, but you gave it your all." He laid his hand on my shoulder and smiled. "That calls for a special dinner," he said, and turned towards his kitchen where we spent a pleasurable evening over delicious seafood.

Silver moonlight broke through the clouds, illuminating the room as we dug into delightful Chilean sea bass in white wine and butter sauce. It had been a long time since we'd seen each other and we had a lot to catch up on. We talked for hours about the changes in our lives, about our spiritual views, and our hopes for the planet.

I slept deeply and awoke to the smell of freshly brewed coffee; raindrops were washing the window of my room. Later, we sat at the kitchen table drinking a cup of coffee, and then I helped Dana load the workshop material in his car. As Dana clicked in his seatbelt, he turned to me and said, "One cup of coffee won't do it. Let's go to First Cup for a second cup."

We drove up the street and parked in front of First Cup, a charming coffee shop filled with locals up early on a Saturday morning discussing the fate of the world. A few spaces were available, and we slid into a polished oak booth. We both had fresh blueberry scones, which energized us, and after a few last-minute sips of fresh dark coffee, we paid the bill, thanked the owners, and headed to the cabin. It was a smooth ride through small towns, places I had never seen. It is always a blessing to see small towns for the first time, with a fresh eye. Light rain was falling, washing the narrow rural roads, as we drove in peaceful silence.

The cabin, surrounded by a serene oak forest, was a one-story wooden building with large windows, one on each side of the brown front door. Excitement and anticipation bubbled inside me as Dana pulled into the cabin parking lot and we got out of the car. Morning sunlight led us to the cabin entrance. I stood on the porch in front of the cabin door and turned back to look at the forest. I took a long deep breath of fresh, crisp forest air. I felt grateful to be surrounded by such natural beauty and majestic oak trees.

We entered the cabin, a large room with a dark wooden floor. At first, it seemed to be empty except for three shelves with a few books on the wall to the right. Then I heard the low voices of the others that were standing there in small groups—several people had already arrived; a few were sitting on the floor, others were leaning against the walls. The lit fire in the fireplace opposite the front door filled the cabin with soothing warmth.

I spread my blanket on the floor near to the fireplace and sat there quietly, allowing my senses to acclimatize to my surroundings. I noticed the brown leather-covered notebook on top of three other books in front of Dana and waited quietly for everyone else to take their places. The other participants spread out their blankets and rugs

Chapter Eight

and sat down, arranging their rattles and other icons around them. We were a group of people eager to learn and practice shamanism. Some I was meeting for the first time, others were familiar faces from previous workshops. It felt great to be around people who shared my excitement and eagerness to explore non-ordinary experiences.

Dana sat with his legs crossed on a gray and red Navajo blanket with yellow strips and lit a dark purple candle, all the while softly chanting shamanic songs. I closed my eyes and meditated to Dana's chants. Soon, other voices joined in with the chanting, timidly at first, creating remarkable sounds that fused together like a soft breeze.

When the last song was over, Dana, sitting erect, opened his eyes and with a gentle smile scanned the group, stopping sometimes to read expressions, and smiling and nodding when he saw a familiar face.

"Good morning," he said eventually. "My name is Dana and I will be your facilitator this weekend. Welcome to the Advanced Shamanic Divination workshop. Would you please introduce yourselves. Who would like to start?"

There were twenty-one people in the cabin, many of them from across the East Coast; others had come from Florida. I was the only one from the Mid-West. Yet we all shared same purpose. Dana then gave a short introduction to shamanic divination.

"Divination is a way of revealing the truth, a way to a deeper understanding of events and circumstances surrounding a situation or person. In certain societies outside the West, divining continues to play an important role, revealing what is hidden, easing anxiety, and helping people come to terms with challenging circumstances that demand the implementation of difficult decisions. It is also often used to understand the meaning of dreams and visions. Divination has always been an integral part of shamanism. Participants in a divination workshop have the opportunity to engage in journeys for each other as well as for themselves, and to acquire experience in using several proven shamanic methods."

The room was silent as we took in what he said.

"In divination, the role of the shaman is to mediate, to act as middle-man," Dana continued. "By exploring and providing an initial reading and interpretation, the shaman allows the seeker to avoid projecting personal wants and desires. One of the typical tasks of the shaman is to journey into non-ordinary reality in order to acquire answers to questions, both at the request of others and for oneself. In your continuing search to become persons of divine knowledge, I will teach you how to connect with divine creation—with nature—as shamans have practiced from time immemorial. You will interact with plants as well as with animal species, you will use quartz crystals, and you will seek and receive revelatory knowledge from visionary sources."

Red World

Dana paused and reached for his drum, a large round wooden frame with tanned leather stretched over it. He griped the drum with his left hand, and in his right hand held a wooden beater with a black cloth ball on top. He started gently beating the drum. I instantly dove down to the Lower World to meet my Power Animals, my spirit helpers.

Warm, clear water greeted me as I stood at the edge of the large hole at the bottom of the ocean. I swiftly dove through the hole onto the water slide and slipped down to the small round water pool in the cave. I stepped out of the pool and went through the open Hobbit-sized arched door. The magical forest's refreshing misty air blew softly on my face, and only a few sunbeams broke through the thick layer of long pine needles. Bear was sitting on the lush green grass, his head resting on his two front paws. He lifted his head and he looked at me with great kindness and wisdom. I was overjoyed to see Bear, his soft snow-white fur glistening in the sunlight.

I didn't want to leave this fairytale place, but I had a journey to make and Bear was to be my guide. I settled myself on his thick white furry back and we soared gently up into the forest and on towards the beach. Bear's ability to fly never ceased to amaze me; huge as he was, he was so light when he flew, carrying me effortlessly to my destination. He descended near Hilla's feet and sat on the white soft sand at the water's edge, just where the waves lose their strength and retreat to the open sea.

Hilla sat on the beach, her back straight, her jet-black hair spilling over her shoulders like a waterfall. She did not acknowledge me, but somehow I knew she was aware of my presence and the purpose of my visit. She gazed out at the ocean and watched Dolphin cavorting in the clear green water.

A few minutes passed in silence. Her long dark olive fingers played in the sand as if she was looking for jewels. Then she looked at me with her beautiful almond-shaped eyes, smiled, and reached out her hand to rest it lovingly on Bear's head.

"Bear will carry you to the Upper World," she said. "Divining is a topic you should discuss with Elijah." Then she closed her eyes, crossed her hands over her chest, and went back to watching Dolphin.

Once more I jumped on Bear's back and grabbed his fur. He signaled me to get ready, and then we flew upwards through the thick layer of white clouds to the familiar soft white cotton-like realm of the Upper World. I walked towards the white palace a step or two ahead of Bear.

Elijah was standing at the giant gates waiting for us. We stopped a few steps in front of him.

"This time we will not enter the garden," he said and turned to walk around the tall wall to the right.

After a short silent walk Elijah stopped and raised his hand. I stopped too, wondering what was next. He turned to face us and signaled for us to follow him. I looked around me, but all I could see was a milky-white fog. We were to leave the white layer! I gasped. I'd never left the White World to travel to another. Still, I knew that with Elijah, this would be a wonderful journey. This time, Bear came to me and waited patiently for me to climb on his back. We followed Elijah as he raised his head and hands upward and flew straight up.

We passed several planets, traveling through vibrant layers of different colors. We eventually landed on the last planet—the red one. I was beyond astonished! I looked around me. My senses were filled by the presence of a very strong red color, radiating a power I had never seen or experienced before. It felt as if I was in the heart of a intense fire that was not hot and that made no sound, but which was alive, in motion. It was the complete opposite of the peacefulness of the White World. The White World was a motionless world; the Red World was one of endless flowing movement.

Elijah stood there, calmly watching me, waiting for me to recover. Once I had, we walked on this soft, caressing yet powerful red surface. At one point, Elijah stopped and sat down on what appeared to be a big stone. All around us was steeped in a magnificent, profound red. Bear seemed unaffected by the red surroundings and stood quietly next to me. I waited to see what would happen next. The effect of this powerful silence and the energy of the red were incredible! I felt humble yet fearless, and strong emotions coursed through my body. I knew I had to be patient and wait for Elijah to explain the purpose of the journey to the Red World.

After a while, he turned to me. His dark eyes, shining like two rare black diamonds, bored into the core of my being.

"What do you see?" he asked.

I was taken aback; all around me there was nothing but shades of red.

"All I see is red." I said, after what seemed like hours.

Elijah smiled radiantly and looked up, then said, "Look straight at it—right through it. Look not only with your eyes."

I looked up. I thought I understood what he meant.

"Humans normally look *at* an object," Elijah continued. "Humans use their eyes and mind to analyze everything around them and form an image out of it. That is your natural sense of seeing. However, looking through an object is not a common way of observing. Using this method, you should look not with your eyes and the mind, but with your soul, using it to overcome the limitations of your mind and the three-dimensional world. Only then can you genuinely experience the full meaning of seeing, feeling, and being an integral part of that which you look at. Only then can you connect to the object's soul." He fell silent, glanced at me for a second, and then shut his eyes.

I looked straight up into the misty red, allowing myself to be absorbed by this powerful color, trying to become part of it, to unite with it, to be one with my entire surroundings. I stood there, feeling myself become gradually extinct, allowing the red to take me over, to consume me. Slowly, I began to feel myself melting. It was as if I was losing all sense of myself, as my body and mind became organic parts of that immense red universe.

"What do you see?" he asked.
I was taken aback; all around me there was nothing but shades of red.
"All I see is red." I said, after what seemed like hours.
Elijah smiled radiantly and looked up, then said, "Look straight at it—right through it. Look not only with your eyes."

"At the End You Will Reach the Beginning"

It was the most glorious vision I had never seen in my whole life. Red serpent-like shapes floated in a huge circle that opened up in the red expanse right above my head. Astonishment washed over me. This circle and those twisting forms were beyond my ken. I had never seen such images. I couldn't tear my eyes away; it was a hypnotic revelation.

I thought that Elijah would explain it and tell me what would happen next, but he said nothing. He just sat there on the stone with his eyes shut, his head bowed towards his chest. He gave no sign that he intended to help me understand. The writhing forms in the red circle looked like headless serpents floating in a red liquid, wrapping around each other, yet never touching one another.

"What should I understand?" I asked, knowing that the information would only come when the time was right.

Then, suddenly I heard a deep vibrating voice: "We have done an experiment."

I knew it wasn't Elijah's voice. This voice was different. It could only have come from that red circle up above me. I looked at Elijah. He just sat there on the rock, his eyes shut, not moving. He and the stone were as one. Stunned, I turned back to look up towards the red. It took me a while before I could say anything.

"What experiment?" I eventually asked. "What does it mean? Who are you?"

"We are the Creator. We are the divine, the source of all, the love," answered the voice. "We created the universe, the planets, and the life upon them."

I was speechless. Here I was, on the Red World talking to the Creator of it all.

"We have made an experiment," the voice continued, "an experiment in creating different organisms with intellect that can endlessly evolve on a single planet. We formed the human race on planet Earth. We shaped human beings in our own form. In your core being, you are like us, but with restricted threads."

Puzzled, I hesitated, but then I asked, "DNA threads?"

"Yes," answered the voice instantly. "With a limited number of threads so you will be able to recreate and evolve in a whole different direction."

"What direction? For what purpose?" I asked.

"We wanted to create a self-sustaining planet that had a limited life span, one on which humans and nature would coexist, where the life of all living beings is in a natural cycle. We wanted to see if this way of living could develop and be sustained without us, the Creator, to intervene and control. If this experiment succeeded, we would do the same on other planets."

"Was the experiment successful?" I asked.

It was a while before the voice replied. "We failed. Humankind is heading for complete extinction. We observed you and saw that the more you developed, the more you lost touch with us, with who you are. As you progressed, you became more destructive towards yourselves and the natural world around you. We created you as a pure and integral part of nature; you are now very far from this pure state. It is as if humans and nature cannot be together on the same planet."

"What will happen next?" I asked. "What's the plan now?"

"Humans are still missing the ability to see without eyes, to see beyond the three dimensions. Soon, however, humans will be ready to see us and we will appear."

"Some can see beyond, but very few people can feel or see you," I replied.

Chapter Eight

"Indeed, and that is part of the experiment," the voice responded. "As time goes on, more and more souls will be able to connect with us, while on Earth. As you know, the whole universe functions in cycles—so does your world. We will not let you destroy yourselves. We must intervene at the right stage to bring your whole existence into a state of complete serenity, where all forms of living—natural and human—sync in one cycle, back to the way in which it all started. The human race is about to learn about us, about the experiment and its purpose. Then we will guide humankind to the end, to where all living forms live in harmony, where all cycles complete one another."

"That will be our end?" I asked.

"Yes," answered the voice. "At the end you will reach the beginning."

~~~—The End—~~~

Thank you for reading!

Dear Reader,

I hope you have enjoyed Walking with Elijah, The Fable of a Life Journey and a Fulfilled Soul.

As an author, I love feedbacks. Candidly, you are the reason that I wrote about my life journey. So, kindly, tell me what you liked, what you loved, even what you didn't like. I'd love to hear from you. You can write me at: doobie.shemer@gmail.com and visit me on the web at: http://www.doobieshemer.com.

Lastly, I would like to ask you a favor. As you may know, book reviews can be tough to obtain these days. You, the reader, have the power to help others discover this book.

If you have the time, please share your opinion using this link to my author page on Amazon: https://amazon.com/author/doobieshemer

Thank you so much for reading Walking with Elijah, The Fable of a Life Journey and a Fulfilled Soul and for spending your time with me.

Gratefully,

Doobie Shemer

Also by Doobie Shemer:

Sprouted Soul: Whole-Souled Poems

Is a compilation of heartfelt poems,
For inner peace, for times of grief,
For gratifying bliss, for emerging belief,
For soothing your soul, for seasons of fall,
For rising hopes when struggling to cope.
To nurture, to heal wounded soul,
To enlighten mystical love, to awaken your call.

http://sproutedsoul.net

Connect with Doobie:

http://walkingwithelijah.com/

https://www.facebook.com/Walking.With.Elijah.the.Book

https://twitter.com/Doobie_Shemer

http://www.pinterest.com/DoobieShemer/walking-with-elijah/

Copyright © 2014 by Doobie Shemer
All rights reserved.
ISBN-13: 978-0-9913494-4-9
ISBN-10: 099134944X
Library of Congress Control Number: TXu 1-919-061

www.ingramcontent.com/pod-product-compliance
Lightning Source LLC
Chambersburg PA
CBHW042053290426
44110CB00006B/168